COGNITIVE PROCESSES

MELVIN MANIS

The University of Michigan

BROOKS/COLE PUBLISHING COMPANY
Belmont, California

A Division of Wadsworth Publishing Company, Inc.

To my parents, Alex and Hanna Manis

Third printing: August   1968

L. C. Cat. Card No.: 66–18122

Printed in the United States of America

SERIES FOREWORD

Basic Concepts in Psychology was conceived as a series of brief paperback volumes constituting a beginning textbook in psychology. Several unique advantages arise from publishing individual chapters as separate volumes rather than under a single cover. Each book or chapter can be written by an author identified with the subject matter of the area. New chapters can be added, individual chapters can be revised independently, and, possibly, competitive chapters can be provided for controversial areas. Finally, to a degree, an instructor of the beginning course in psychology can choose a particular set of chapters to meet the needs of his students.

Probably the most important impetus for the series came from the fact that a suitable textbook did not exist for the beginning courses in psychology at the University of Michigan—Psychology 100 (Psychology as a Natural Science) and Psychology 101 (Psychology as a Social Science). In addition, no laboratory manual treated both the natural science and social science problems encountered in the first laboratory course, Psychology 110.

For practical rather than ideological reasons, the initial complement of authors comes from the staff of the University of Michigan. Coordination among geographically dispersed authors seems needlessly difficult, and the diversity of points of view in the Department of Psychology at Michigan makes the danger of parochialism quite small.

Each author in the Basic Concepts in Psychology Series has considerable freedom. He has been charged to devote approximately half of his resources to elementary concepts and half to topics of special interest and emphasis. In this way, each volume will reflect the personality and viewpoint of the author while presenting the subject matter usually found in a chapter of an elementary textbook.

PREFACE

In recent years psychologists have become increasingly concerned with the study of cognitive processes. Perhaps the most hopeful aspect of this trend is the stimulation it has provided for new and more searching experimental techniques. This book is intended to provide an introductory overview of cognitive functioning, with particular emphasis on those areas that have proven amenable to laboratory investigation. This implicit bias has led to an emphasis on the American scientific literature; the instructor may wish to supplement this text for a fuller discussion of European trends in cognitive research.

I would like to express my appreciation to Austin Jones, Edward L. Walker, and Robert B. Zajonc for helpful comments.

CONTENTS

Series Foreword   iii

Preface   iv

Chapter 1:   Introduction   1
      The Organization and Content of This Book   2

Chapter 2:   Learning   4
      Reinforcement   5
      Programmed Learning   12

Chapter 3:   Memory   18
      Forgetting and Disuse   19
      Forgetting and Organization   21
      Organization and Coding   22
      Organization and Memory Distortion   24
      Forgetting and Active Changes in the Memory Trace   26
      Memory and Response Competition   27
      Motivation and Memory   30
      The Zeigarnik Effect   32

Chapter 4:   Going Beyond What Is Given   35
      Stimulus Generalization   35
      Response Generalization   39
      Generalization and Cognition   40
      Concreteness and Abstraction   41

Chapter 5:   Concept Formation   44
      Continuity versus Discontinuity   47
      Reversal and Nonreversal Shifts   51
      Strategies in Concept Attainment   52

Chapter 6:   Psychology of Language   56
      B. F. Skinner   56
      C. E. Osgood   59
      General Semantics   65
      Syntactics   67
      The Statistical Approach to Language   70
      Interpreting Persuasive Messages   71

Chapter 7:   Thinking and Problem Solving   80
      Learning and Thinking   81

Chapter 7:   Thinking and Problem Solving—Continued
                  Thinking and Insight   81
                  Thought and Language   85
                  The Whorfian Hypothesis   86
                  The Representational Nature of Thought   91
                  Representation of the Future   93
                  Representation as an Aid in Problem Solving   94
                  Problem Solving and the Fixation of Incorrect
                      Responses   96
                  Restructuring the Problem Situation   100
                  Thought and Motivation   102
Chapter 8:   Creativity   105
                  Age and Creativity   107
                  Stimulating Creativity in Groups   109
                  Stimulating Originality   110
                  Creativity as the Formation of New Associative
                      Linkages   111

            References   113
            Index   119

In a sense, this book will deal with matters quite familiar to you. Such processes as learning, remembering, communicating, and thinking have been directly experienced by all of us; and yet we are only now beginning to gain a scientific understanding of them. Our very familiarity with these cognitive processes may impede progress, for there is a great temptation to substitute direct experience and intuitive understanding for the sort of cautious and "hardheaded" inquiry that has typically led to scientific advances. After all, if "it is perfectly obvious that thinking is all a matter of association," it is difficult to see just where the problem lies. Why bother to question or conduct experiments if the ultimate conclusion seems so self-evident?

One reason, of course, is the fact that some of our most "reasonable" and unquestioned assumptions may ultimately prove to be incorrect. For example, our direct and immediate impression of the world we inhabit would hardly lead to the conclusion that the earth is round; nor is untutored "common sense" likely to suggest that the change from day to night is due to the earth's rotation, for it seems so obvious to the naive observer that the sun passes around the earth, despite the astronomer's contentions to the contrary. Analogously, while psychologists are interested in explanations that are intuitively reasonable and compelling, they are well aware of the dangers that accompany such conclusions and prefer, when possible, that their assertions reflect more than just "common sense." Stated more positively, psychologists, along with other scientists, seek conclusions based on evidence that is *public* (can be viewed by others) and *reproducible* (the relevant observations may be repeated).

Consequently, psychologists interested in cognitive processes do not rely solely upon a subjective assessment (or introspection) of their own thought processes. While it is clear that psychologists often derive scientific hunches from their private musings and self-observations, the evidence ultimately considered in evaluating psychological theories, as you shall see, typically consists of observations concerning the behavior of others.

For example, suppose that my personal experiences and self-observation have convinced me that things learned slowly and with difficulty are generally not forgotten, while things learned with ease are often forgotten rather quickly. To test this idea in an adequate fashion, it would be necessary to collect a variety of materials that differ in their ease of learning; in a crude experiment, some people might be faced with the problem of learning a simple poem, perhaps suitable for a third-grade reader, while others might attempt to memorize a poem of equal length taken, let us say, from the works of T. S. Eliot. Our subjects would study these materials until they could recite their assigned passages without error; some time after this learning session—perhaps a week or two later—we might call them back again and without warning see how much they could recall of the material they had learned. If my hypothesis were correct, we would expect that the people who had learned the more difficult passage from Eliot would show better recall than those assigned the children's poem. Until evidence of this type could be produced, my hypothesis concerning the relation between learning speed and retention would at best be regarded as an interesting (and perhaps plausible) idea. However, if repeated experiments like the one described above were to show (as they generally do) that we are most successful in recalling materials relatively *simple* to learn, we should be forced to reject my hypothesis, despite its apparent "reasonableness" and "good sense." Or we could, on the other hand, modify the hypothesis, perhaps by asserting that lessons that are difficult to learn tend to be easily recalled only if these tasks involve motor skills like swimming and bicycle riding; in brief, perhaps our initial generalization does not apply to the learning of poetry. However, before accepting this somewhat altered hypothesis, we would again strive to evaluate our theory by observing the behavior of others in experimental tests similar to the one described above. Thus, we might repeat our experiment using learning tasks that require the acquisition of *motor skills*, rather than verbal associations; as before, we would train two groups of subjects—one on a difficult task and one on a simple problem—and we would then assess the speed with which these learned skills were forgotten, following the original training experience.

The main point to all this is the fact that modern psychologists insist on the necessity for empirical verification. As a result, they tend to be somewhat skeptical of generalizations mainly based on informal observations and personal intuitions. Psychologists strive, whenever possible, to obtain quantifiable data that may bear on the truth or falsity of their scientific propositions.

THE ORGANIZATION AND CONTENT OF THIS BOOK

This book will consider a variety of cognitive processes, starting with learning and memory, and then gradually broadening to deal with the more complex processes of generalization, concept formation, language, thinking, and creativity. The main feature that these areas hold in common is an emphasis upon intelligent nonreflexive behavior, which typically serves to facilitate man's ability to cope successfully with his environment.

Other themes deserve special mention here. Most important perhaps is the concept of generalization—the idea that humans, and animals too, are often capable of generalizing from a limited set of experiences. This capacity to "go beyond what is (explicitly) given" may be considered an important hallmark of cognition, for in its absence only a limited range of "intelligent" behavioral processes seems possible. Moreover, generalizability underlies our capacity to adapt our actions quickly to newly encountered situations; through generalization, we are often successful in meeting new contingencies.

Finally, we should note that the topics in this book are treated roughly in order of increasing complexity. *Learning* and *memory* are relatively simple processes that play an important role in determining the course of *generalization* and *concept formation.* Similarly, these latter processes are helpful in understanding certain aspects of *language behavior,* which in turn plays a vital role in *thinking, problem solving,* and *creativity.* While these links are not always made explicit, the final structure of this book was based partly upon them.

LEARNING

One of the most striking aspects of human behavior is its plasticity; this term refers to man's almost infinite capacity to adapt his behavior to diverse conditions. In contrast to more primitive forms of life, man shows a startling variety of behaviors, depending largely upon the circumstances that surround him; he does not react in a stereotyped manner when faced with new problems, but is instead strikingly successful in his ability to alter his actions to meet the demands of his environment.

In trying to achieve a more adequate understanding of this adaptability, psychologists have intensively studied the learning process. We should hasten to add that the term "learning," as it is used by psychologists, includes far more than the acquisition of knowledge and techniques that you may associate with formal education. Instead, it is typically defined as a *relatively permanent behavior change that results from practice*. This definition does not differentiate between "intellectual" forms of learning, such as occur in the classroom, and the learning of such simple skills as the tying of one's shoelaces. While there are clearly important differences between the two cases, the psychologist typically assumes that similar processes are at work and strives, so far as is possible, to explain the more complex cases of learning in the same terms that he uses in discussing more rudimentary instances. He adopts this stance in the interests of *simplicity* and *generality*.

Scientific theories are generally deemed successful if they use a limited number of simple but powerful generalizations to explain what have previously appeared to be baffling complex phenomena. Thus, we would ideally like to find a limited set of general propositions that would enable us to explain a wide diversity of observed facts, just as the axioms of geometry may be used to deduce a variety of theorems. We shall follow this approach as far as we can, both in explaining the learning process and in applying the principles of learning to account for more complex phenomena such as language and thinking. We should hasten to add, however, that the higher mental processes cannot, at present, be adequately explained in terms of a few general propositions, and hence we shall continue to introduce new terms and concepts as they are needed.

The material that follows in this chapter will provide an introduction to learning concepts and phenomena that seem most applicable to an understanding of complex cognitive processes. A more complete treatment of this material may be found in another volume in this series (Walker, *Conditioning and Instrumental Learning*, 1966).

In the language of the contemporary learning theorist, learning occurs when the individual associates a new *response* with a given *stimulus* situation. For example, after awkward trial and error, a child may learn that when given the stimulus "2 + 2," he should respond "4." By convention, the term "stimulus" is often used in a very broad sense; the stimulus may be virtually any environmental element or setting that has a systematic effect upon behavior. Thus, the presence of father (stimulus) will typically lead the little boy to use the word "Daddy" (response) more frequently than he does in situations where father is not present. And, after learning, the stimulus "2 + 2" systematically elicits the response "4" from the child.

A convenient way of representing the changes that take place during learning is the *habit-family hierarchy* diagrammed in Figure 1. This

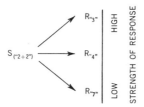

Figure 1

Hypothetical habit-family hierarchy in response to stimulus "2 + 2."

scheme is intended to convey the notion that the stimulus (S) of "2 + 2" tends to elicit a variety of responses (R), some more strongly than others. Thus, early in the learning of "2 + 2" the child's predominant response may be "3," which we have designated as R"3." As learning progresses, however, this response tends to become weaker (less probable), and the R"4" response, which was originally rather weak, gains in strength until it is the most likely response of all.

REINFORCEMENT

We are now in a position to ask about the all-important factors that produce these changes in the habit-family hierarchy. In brief, under what conditions will the correct response, "4," rise to the top of the hierarchy? While psychologists do not unanimously agree in their answers to this question, it is clear that if the event (or events) which *follows* the individual's response is a positive experience (parental approval, for example), the response will typically gain in strength; that is, when the appropriate stimulus is subsequently presented, the rewarded response will appear with increasing speed. On the other hand, if a given response is followed by unpleasant events (disapproval), or if it has no discernible effect, either positive or negative, it will generally lose its strength and eventually disappear as a response to the stimulus. When a response is weakened because of its negative consequences, the change is the result of *punishment*. When a response is weakened because it has neither positive nor negative consequences, *experimental extinction* has occurred. Thus, if a child's parents refuse to respond to requests phrased in baby-talk, this response pattern will soon lose its strength (that is, appear less and less frequently) and undergo extinction.

Summing up, then, the strengthening or weakening of a given stimulus-response association will partly depend on the *effects* that the response produces; more technically, these effects are referred to as *reinforcers*. A positive reinforcer is thus an effect (or outcome) that the individual seeks, and it serves to strengthen the association between the preceding response and the stimulus situation present when the response was performed. A negative reinforcer, on the other hand, refers to an effect (or outcome) that the individual would prefer to avoid, and generally leads to a weakening of the response that has preceded it.

Does *all* learning depend upon the presence of reinforcers? Can a stimulus-response association be formed in the absence of a reinforcement? This issue has plagued learning theorists for several decades. In part, the answer depends upon the way in which we define reinforcement. For example, it is perfectly clear that learning can take place in situations where there is no external agent (for example, experimenter or teacher) to reinforce the learner. Thus, the student may read in an elementary psychology text that Wundt founded the first psychology laboratory in Leipzig; on the basis of his reading, the student may be quite capable of responding successfully when he is subsequently asked test questions concerning this aspect of psychology. To account for this apparent demonstration of learning without reinforcement, an advocate of the reinforcement concept might argue that in the past our student has been reinforced by his teachers for mastering his readings, and he thus automatically practices this skill when faced with new reading material. However, this approach weakly assumes that the learning of today's reading material is primarily based upon the reinforcements of yesterday's responses.

Our analysis suggests that learning may occur in the absence of reinforcers, although the issue cannot be satisfactorily decided because human subjects often "reinforce themselves" without the experimenter's intervention. That is, in our reading example there is always the possibility that the learner achieves some subjective satisfaction through the insights that he gains as he progresses through his text, or by asking himself questions and then checking the accuracy of his responses; if this were true (and the possibility cannot be easily ruled out), the learning that occurs in this setting might be attributed to the effects of self-administered reinforcement.

To overcome this type of experimental limitation, many researchers have sought to evaluate the role of reinforcement in animal learning, where there seem to be fewer complications. In a famous experiment by Blodgett (1929), a group of hungry rats were permitted to explore a maze that did *not* have a food reward in the goal box. Another group of rats was placed in the maze when food was present in the goal box. While this second group readily learned the maze, showing a steady decrease in errors (that is, entries into blind alleys), the unrewarded group showed little improvement. After several days of unrewarded training, a food reward was finally introduced into the goal box for the group that had been exploring without reinforcement; for some of these rats the rewards were introduced on the third day of training, and for others on the seventh day. The results are shown in Figure 2. Note that the intro-

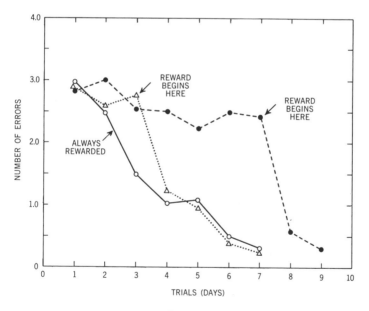

Figure 2

Example of latent learning. Following the delayed introduction of rewards, maze performance soon reaches level achieved by animals consistently rewarded throughout training trials. (Adapted from J. Deese, The Psychology of Learning. *New York: McGraw-Hill Book Co., Inc., 1958. Data from Blodgett, 1929.)*

duction of reward resulted in a rapid decrease of errors, and that the animals not initially rewarded quickly attained the same performance level as the animals that had always been rewarded. This effect has been termed "latent learning"; it has been interpreted as an indication that the animals were learning about the maze during the unrewarded trials even though they continued to make many errors. Presumably, however, this learning remained "latent" and was not clearly apparent until the food rewards were later introduced.

Extrapolating from data of this sort (there have been numerous related experiments), many psychologists have concluded that learning may indeed take place even when there is no obvious reinforcement following the performance of a response. The Blodgett experiment leads to the further point that what has been *learned* may not be directly reflected in *performance* (that is, overt behavior); thus, even though Blodgett's unrewarded rats apparently learned a good deal about the structure of their maze, they did not reveal this knowledge (by avoiding the blind alleys) until the food rewards were introduced. This distinction between learning and performance holds true at the human level too. For example, an individual's performance in a highly demanding athletic event may not only reflect his learned skill, but will also be affected by such variables as his level of motivation, and the magnitude of the prize (if any) for which he is competing.

KNOWLEDGE OF RESULTS

In studies of human learning, it is often unnecessary to present the learner with any concrete reward; if there is motivation to improve, considerable learning may be achieved if we simply give the learner periodic feedback about how well he is doing. Psychologists refer to this as providing "knowledge of results." Thorndike (1932b) has shown that if a blindfolded person attempts to draw a 3-inch line, his performance will be rather poor and will not show improvement even though he is allowed to "practice," *if he is prevented from seeing the results of his efforts.* If, however, following each attempt, the experimenter measures the line that is drawn and says "right" whenever the line deviates from the 3-inch standard by less than one eighth of an inch, and "wrong" on all other trials, the subject will show rapid improvement. Studies of this sort clearly indicate the importance of adequate knowledge of results in guiding learning. This principle proved particularly helpful in training gunners during the Second World War. When a gun has been fired, it is sometimes difficult to tell whether or not the target has been hit. By developing various training devices to give the gunner feedback about whether or not he had hit his target, it was possible to improve greatly the effectiveness of gunnery training programs.

DELAY OF FEEDBACK

Studies concerned with the effects of reinforcement upon animal behavior have uniformly shown that delay of reinforcement following a correct response slows learning, and may indeed prevent it (Grice, 1948). Analogously, some psychologists feel that knowledge of results is most effective if it is presented immediately after the learner's response. However, the data are far from clear. While it is reasonable to assume that man's ability to speak to himself may enable him to bridge effectively the gap between his overt response and the eventual feedback or reinforcement, this mechanism may be difficult to employ when the response to be learned cannot readily be "stored" in verbal equivalents. For example, in teaching French we may ask for the English equivalent of the word *livre* and then wait, say, 15 seconds before telling our student whether his answer was right or wrong. This delay may have little impact upon learning speed, however, since he can inwardly "rehearse" the answer he gave until the feedback is given. In contrast, consider a dart-throwing situation where the learner is prevented from seeing the results of his throws and where he does not have a readily available linguistic means of storing and recalling the precise muscular components of a given throw. In such a situation we may indeed find that delayed feedback leads to impaired learning.

In discussing the effects of delayed rewards on learning, it is important to consider the individual's activities between the time of his response and the teacher's (or experimenter's) feedback. The available research suggests that delay of reward will be most detrimental to learning if, prior to the experimenter's feedback, the learner has engaged in additional activities similar to the behaviors he is learning. Thus, Ammons suggested (1956) that "Knowledge of performance serves as a reward, and what is rewarded is the ongoing behavior at the time of reward. When we delay knowledge we simply decrease the possibility that the behavior which we intend to reward is actually rewarded, and increase the possibility that some relatively irrelevant response is rewarded." [1] While this effect can be reduced if the learner is capable of symbolically reinstating his original response (the one being rewarded), it is likely that forgetting will impair covert reinstatement if, following each practice trial, our learner engages in other actions closely resembling the responses to be learned. For example, Lorge and Thorndike (1935) taught subjects to throw a ball at a target that was not visible

[1] From Ammons, R. B. "Effects of Knowledge of Performance: A Survey and Tentative Theoretical Formulation." *J. Gen. Psych.*, 1956, *54*, 279–299. Quoted with permission of the publisher.

to them. For single throws, performance was essentially unaffected by delayed knowledge of results. However, when the subjects were required to make a second throw before receiving feedback on their preceding attempt, performance was impaired.

Careful consideration of delayed reward (or feedback) suggests that two mechanisms may impair performance. One of these, as discussed above, is the notion that when the reward finally appears, it may strengthen the response just previously performed, rather than the response actually instrumental in obtaining the reward. The second problem is motivation. If the learner is forced to respond for long stretches of time without knowing how he is doing, his motivation may flag and he may lose interest in the task.

MECHANISTIC VERSUS COGNITIVE EFFECTS OF REWARD

While there is little disagreement among psychologists concerning the empirical effects of verbal rewards such as "Good" or "That's right" in effecting learning, these data have been the subject of several interpretations. Thorndike asserted in his *Law of Effect* that rewards operated in an automatic fashion to strengthen the responses that preceded them; moreover, this strengthening was said to be independent of the learner's "understanding" of the situation. In contrast to this view, a more cognitive approach might emphasize the information-giving aspects of a reward (it simply informs the learner that a given response has been correct), as opposed to the reward's "stamping in" characteristics. Note that both of these accounts are consistent with much of the evidence thus far presented; for example, they would both be consistent with the fact that rewarded responses tend to be repeated, and that learning is virtually impossible in the absence of knowledge of results. While most laymen might prefer the cognitive interpretation because of its greater compatibility with a humanistic conception of man, scientific conclusions are not ideally based on considerations of this type, and hence several lines of experimentation have been pursued in an attempt to gain more adequate understanding.

Following Thorndike's mechanistic line of thought, many experimenters have been concerned with the effectiveness of rewards in incidental learning situations. In these studies, the experimental setting is such that the subjects are not consciously motivated to repeat responses termed "correct." For example, Postman and Adams (1954) employed what was presented as an extrasensory perception (ESP) task. Their subjects were shown a series of words and were to guess the number between 1 and 10 which the experimenters had paired with each word. After each guess, subjects were told whether they had been right or wrong; however, since the experimenters were not truly interested in ESP, the feedback followed a prearranged pattern and did not depend upon the accuracy of the subjects' guesses. Following the first presentation of the list, the words were repeated, with the subjects again instructed to guess the associated numbers—this time without any feedback from the experimenter. In responding to this second presentation, subjects were instructed that the word-number pairings would be randomly changed, so that a number that had initially been "correct" for a given word would not necessarily be correct on the second presentation of the word list. If rewards operated in a purely mechanistic fashion to strengthen the stimulus-response associations that they followed, we would expect to find many repeated responses to words that had initially been followed by reward ("right") and relatively few repetitions on items that had been followed by punishment ("wrong"). On the other hand, according to a cognitive interpretation of reward, we would not expect this pattern of results, since the subjects had been led to believe that the feedback they had initially received could not be used to guide their future performance, because many of the word-number pairs were presumably to be changed. Several experiments of this sort have been conducted to date, and the results have generally shown the trends predicted by Thorndike's mechanistic theory. That is, on the second presentation of the word list, repeated responses have typically occurred on items that had initially been associated with reward. Moreover, when asked to recall the number responses that they originally gave to each word, subjects have been more successful in recalling the rewarded responses than the responses that were initially unrewarded.

A second line of research, bearing on the mechanistic-versus-cognitive interpretation of reinforcement, has been concerned with the effects of "awareness" on behavior. One of the earliest studies in this tradition was conducted by Greenspoon (1955); subjects in this experiment were simply instructed to say all the words they could think of, without using any phrases or sentences, and without counting. Without telling his subjects that there were any right or wrong responses, Greenspoon attempted to reinforce the use of plural nouns by the simple expedient of saying "mmm-hmmm" whenever a plural was emitted. His results indicated that this procedure led to an increased usage of plural nouns. However, more interesting than this straightforward demonstration of the efficacy of verbal rewards was the fact that when his subjects were questioned at the end of the experimental session, only ten out of seventy-five were able to verbalize the relationship between their responses and the experimenter's reinforcing behavior ("mmm-hmmm"). Moreover, these ten subjects did not respond differently from the sixty-five subjects who were "unaware" of the experimental manipulations, suggesting that the experimenter's subtle verbal rewards had been equally effective regardless of the subjects' "insight" into the situation.

Many more studies of this sort have been conducted to date. The vast majority show that it is indeed possible to alter people's verbal behavior by having the experimenter say such things as "Good," "Right," etc. There is, however, considerable controversy concerning the claims that learning can occur without awareness. For example, it has been argued that in the Greenspoon study and those conducted shortly after it, the post-experimental interview was too brief and superficial, and thus failed to detect awareness on the part of many subjects who did, in fact, have insight into what the experimenter was doing (Spielberger, 1962). These critics have gone on to show that when the subjects' awareness is assessed by a more adequate set of probing questions, a substantially greater proportion are judged to have awareness; even more important, these critics maintain, is the fact that there is generally no evidence that the "truly" unaware subjects have learned. Thus, the critics assert that a careful review of these studies suggests that learning cannot occur without awareness and that previous claims for such a phenomenon have been based on faulty experimentation.

In concluding this discussion, we may tentatively offer the generalization that the mechanistic effects of reinforcement may be most readily demonstrated in situations where the learner's behavior involves the acquisition of stimulus-response associations that are rather arbitrary in origin (as in the mastery of number-word pairs) and not easily summarized by a verbal rule. It seems likely, however, that these mechanistic effects also play an important role in settings where the subject must learn to follow a systematic behavior pattern, despite the above criticisms of Greenspoon's early work. For example, while we have all learned to speak with reasonable grammatical correctness, few of us are aware of the "rules" that govern our choice of words as we participate in a conversation. Thus, we can choose the proper words to create a meaningful sentence, but may be unable to explain why a given word order or verb form was used. Examples of this sort suggest that it may be quite possible for a learner's behavior to be shaped into systematic patterns (presumably through the operation of a reinforcing environment), despite his lack of *awareness* concerning the pattern he has learned to follow.

PROGRAMMED LEARNING: AN APPLICATION OF LEARNING PRINCIPLES

Perhaps the most widely publicized innovation in teaching technology within the past few decades has been the development of programmed learning techniques (also known as the teaching machine). This approach to instruction was introduced by B. F. Skinner in the mid-1950s, although Sidney L. Pressey had worked with a somewhat related device in the 1930s. While Pressey's apparatus was known to facilitate student *learning*, it was mainly designed as an automatic *testing* method, and its merits as a teaching device were held to be incidental. Skinner, on the other hand, was interested in improving instructional practice; in the main, he adapted to the classroom the practices and principles that had developed in the training of laboratory animals.

What do we mean by programmed learning? And how is it related to learning principles? The typical program consists of a carefully ordered series of questions presented one at a time. After writing out his answer to a question, the learner compares his response with the correct answer. If he is right, he goes on to the next question; if he is wrong, he can often arrange for the machine to present the question again, when the entire set has been completed.

The main features of programmed instruction can often be realized without the aid of any "hardware." A good example may be found in the laboratory manual of this series (Lane and Bem, A *Laboratory Manual for the Control and Analysis of Behavior*, 1965). The questions can appear in a simple workbook with space left for the insertion of answers; the correct answers can be printed in another section of the workbook to minimize the temptation to cheat. However, a mechanical presentation of the program may provide certain advantages. For one thing, a machine can be constructed to control cheating. The learner may be unable to write in his response to a question once he has exposed the correct answer. Similarly, the machine may prevent the learner from advancing to the next question until he has attempted the one at hand (if he leaves an item blank and simply proceeds, this fact is automatically recorded, along with all other aspects of his performance). Another advantage of mechanical accessories is that they can often be used in presenting programmed materials to those who cannot read or write. Here, the lessons can be arranged so that the learner may simply push a button in an effort to match one of several answers (given in the form of pictures) with a question (also a picture). Finally, a mechanical gadget may have some motivational value, since levers and buttons may make the learning situation more interesting and attractive, especially to youngsters.

Regardless of the format used for display of the programmed material, several learning principles seem to be particularly pertinent. For one thing, the learner typically gets *immediate feedback* on the correctness of his responses. Immediate knowledge of results is rarely available in the typical classroom; and in the opinion of some critics, this reduces the effectiveness of the teacher's eventual feedback as a reinforcer, and lowers the student's incentive to learn.

A somewhat related feature of programmed instruction is the fact that the student must actively engage in the learning process; he cannot sit back passively, but must work steadily in order to complete his lessons. This insures his participation and attention during the course of learning, although some studies (Goldstein and Gotkin, 1962; Alter and Silverman, 1962) show no difference in final performance between students who actively *write out* their answers, and those who merely read the program.

A final principle incorporated in programmed instruction is *shaping*, or learning by *successive approximations*. By this we mean that a complex skill can often be taught if the component skills are gradually taught in sequence, until the final performance can be emitted as a single act. For example, Skinner taught a pigeon to turn around in a clockwise circle by first reinforcing him for turning his head to the right; later, reinforcements were delivered if the pigeon turned right and took one or two steps in that direction. By successively "demanding" additional components of the complete clockwise turn as a means of gaining reinforcements, the experimenter can eventually induce the pigeon to perform this complicated maneuver in its entirety—a feat that would be rather unlikely to occur without preliminary shaping.

In a similar vein, the sequence of questions is of great importance in programmed instruction. By learning to respond appropriately to the early questions in the program, the student gradually acquires the capacity to answer the later, more difficult problems. There is, however, a difference from the concept of shaping as it applies in the laboratory. In the laboratory the final act includes as components the simpler skills that were strengthened early in the learning sequence, while in programmed instruction, the final performance (on the most difficult items, for example) will rarely include the responses that comprised the early steps. In any case, advocates of programmed instruction have been particularly emphatic on the problem of sequencing the lessons to be presented; Skinner, for example, recommends a program in which the successive steps are related closely enough so that the learner will rarely make an error. The notion here is that through careful sequencing, the skills demanded at any given point in the learning process should have already been developed in the lessons that have gone before. In a sense, this emphasis on a logical sequence of questions as a means of teaching complex subject matter may be thought of as a modern version of the Socratic method, for Socrates employed a similar technique in his teachings. (See Cohen, 1962, for a comparison of programmed learning and Socratic questioning.)

Given this brief introduction, the reader may now wonder about the effectiveness of programmed learning. Effectiveness of a program depends upon how skillfully it is constructed; well-designed programs result from a very long and arduous process of pre-testing and analytical thought. If most of the learners miss a given sequence of questions, the programmer knows that for some reason the students have not been adequately prepared for these materials, and that he must rework the lesson.

In contrast, the classroom teacher may find it more difficult to determine just where a given presentation went astray.

A second consideration is that programmed instruction is most adaptable to subjects that readily lend themselves to a logical presentation; such subjects would include mathematics (especially geometry), physics, and the acquisition of certain simple skills such as may be called for in arithmetic or foreign languages. In contrast, a subject like philosophy or history or American literature is more difficult to program effectively.

A final point is that programmed learning materials permit the learner to go as quickly or as slowly as he wishes, without worrying about the progress of his classmates. While this is generally advantageous, it is also true that in order to design any program, it is necessary to have some specific group of students in mind, in order to capitalize on their existing knowledge and general intellectual skills. This means, for example, that in a program designed for the average fifth-grader, the very gifted child, although he can work at his own rate, may find that the successive steps in the program are boringly small. He may be insulted at the very slow rate of coverage, even though leisurely presentation proves quite effective for the majority of his classmates.

With continued experience in this new field, we will doubtless develop a better understanding of the situations and populations for which programmed instruction is best suited.

SUMMARY

1. Learning is defined as a relatively permanent change in behavior which results from practice. In its simplest form, learning is a process in which the individual associates a new response with a given stimulus; or it may consist of a strengthened association between a stimulus and a response.

2. The *habit-family hierarchy* is a convenient way to represent the changes that take place during learning. The basic notion here is that each stimulus tends to be associated with several alternative responses. As learning progresses, these responses are "reshuffled" so that a response that initially was only weakly associated with the stimulus may become strengthened until it dominates all the other alternatives. Similarly, a response that was initially the individual's dominant reaction to a given stimulus may become weaker.

3. When a response is followed by positive (or pleasurable) consequences, it is said to have been *reinforced*. Responses that are reinforced get stronger; that is, if a stimulus has led to a response which has in turn been reinforced, there will be an increased likelihood that when the stimulus is presented again, the reinforced response will be repeated. In

contrast, a response followed by negative consequences (punishment) is generally weakened. Finally, a stimulus-response association that has become strong as a result of repeated reinforcement will get weaker if the reinforcement is subsequently withheld; this process is called *experimental extinction*.

4. Although learning may occur without obvious reinforcement, what has been learned may not be directly reflected in performance (what the individual actually does). The principle of reinforcement is thus primarily concerned with performance rather than learning.

5. In human learning, considerable improvement may be achieved if the learner is given explicit feedback (knowledge of results) concerning how well he is doing; without knowledge of results, there may be no improvement, even though the individual is given an opportunity to practice.

6. Some psychologists feel that knowledge of results is most effective if it is presented immediately after the learner's response; however, the evidence is not clear on this point. When delayed feedback does impair performance, two possible mechanisms may be at work: (a) When the feedback finally appears, it may affect the response just performed, rather than the response for which the feedback was intended. (b) When people are forced to respond for long periods of time without being told how they are doing, they may lose interest in the task.

7. While there is general agreement concerning the effects of verbal rewards (such as "Good" or "That's right") on behavior, these data may be interpreted in two ways. Thorndike's *Law of Effect* emphasized the automatic strengthening of responses which occurs when they are followed by reinforcement; according to Thorndike, this strengthening occurs whether or not the learner has an appropriate "understanding" of the relationship between his behavior and the appearance of the reward. In contrast to this mechanistic view, some theorists have taken a cognitive position and have emphasized the information-giving aspects of reinforcement. That is, telling a person he is "right" affects his subsequent behavior by enhancing his understanding of what to do in this situation (the verbal reinforcement helps the learner to gain insight about the correct mode of behavior in that particular setting).

8. Programmed learning techniques developed in recent years show interesting similarities to the learning principles developed in the laboratory. In the typical program, the learner responds to a series of questions presented one at a time. After each response, he is given immediate feedback about whether he was right or wrong.

The order and relative difficulty of the various questions presents the programmer with an important problem, for if the student is to respond correctly to the most difficult parts of the program, he must previously have mastered the various skills required. This means that the successive questions in the program should be closely related, so that the learner can proceed successfully from one to the next. This aspect of programmed learning is somewhat related to the technique of *successive approximations*, which is often used in training laboratory animals. Successive approximations refer to the fact that a complex skill can often be mastered most effectively if the component skills are first taught in sequence, until the final performance can be emitted as a single act. By use of this technique, Skinner has succeeded in teaching laboratory animals to engage in activities that would be quite "foreign" to their normal behavioral repertory without the benefit of this preliminary "shaping."

MEMORY

While learning permeates our everyday lives, we are all also quite familiar (sometimes unhappily) with the fact that many things we have learned are too quickly forgotten. Memory and forgetting are, of course, serious practical concerns to all of us, for the successful performance of many tasks depends upon how effectively we can recall and apply the learnings of yesterday. The psychologist is interested in the phenomena of memory too, both because of their practical importance, and because of the theoretical implications that they may hold for an adequate understanding of human intellectual functioning.

In general, we say that forgetting has taken place when we observe that the passage of time is accompanied by a decrement in the performance of some learned activity. For example, although John Jones may have mastered the Gettysburg Address when he studied it as a grade school student, when he tries to recall it now, six years later, he may find that he can no longer recite it in its entirety. The difference between his earlier perfect performance and his present less than perfect performance is due to forgetting.

The scientific study of memory was inaugurated by Ebbinghaus in 1885; his work is important for several reasons. First, it represents what is probably the earliest attempt to carry out quantitative, experimental research on one of the higher mental processes; before his time, objective research had been restricted to the study of sensation. Second, Ebbinghaus's work is important because he devised two techniques still widely employed in the study of memory. In searching for verbal materials relatively "uncontaminated" by earlier association, he invented the *nonsense syllable*, which simply consists of a vowel surrounded by consonants, such as VEK or ZAT or CEV. As subsequent work (Glaze, 1928) has shown, such meaningless syllables do indeed have associations for subjects. But such syllables have nevertheless remained in use, largely because they permit the study of memory in a setting where the materials are relatively unfamiliar, and are but weakly embedded in the subject's cognitive and verbal habits.

In his studies of memory, Ebbinghaus also employed what has come to be known as the *method of savings*. In this method, memory is measured by having the subject relearn, to a point of complete mastery, materials he is trying to retain. By comparing time required for complete relearning with the time required for initial mastery, a "savings score" may be devised. For example, if a list of ten nonsense syllables was originally mastered after one minute of study, but it required only 30 seconds to relearn it to perfection a month later, this represents a savings score of 50 percent, which we attribute to our subject's retention of the initially learned materials.

The method of savings often reveals considerable retention in cases where the subject's inability to recall the original material may suggest that he remembers little, if anything. This is clearly illustrated in a study by Burtt (1941) in which, for a period of time prior to his son's second birthday, he read the boy three passages in Greek from Sophocles' *Oedipus Tyrannus;* six years later, the boy learned these same passages plus several other selections from the same source. While it took 317 repetitions to master the old passages, the new selections required 435 repetitions. Since the old passages were learned in 73 percent of the repetitions required for the new ones, we may conclude that the boy's retention of his early experience resulted in a savings of about 27 percent, even though it is certain that he could have recalled virtually none of this material had he simply attempted to recite the passages from memory, as required by the method of recall.

By studying his own retention for lists of nonsense syllables at varying time intervals after he had learned them, Ebbinghaus discovered what has come to be known as the "forgetting curve." His results have subsequently been replicated by other investigators; they are graphically depicted in Figure 3, which shows that immediately after learning, we forget things rather rapidly, but that with the passage of time, the rate of forgetting becomes slower and slower. This change in the rate of forgetting is reflected in *Jost's Law,* which states that within a given time interval we are more likely to forget memories of recent origin than those derived from long-past experience.

FORGETTING AND DISUSE

Most people think that forgetting results from disuse. They would explain John Jones's inaccurate performance of the Gettysburg Address by noting that he had not practiced this recitation for years and that, as a consequence, the constituent skills and associations had "weakened," something like an unused muscle. As we shall see, the disuse theory is not accepted by most psychologists, mostly because it is too simple and fails to account for many important memory phenomena. Indeed, if we generalize from the phenomenon of experimental extinction, we are led to the expectation that forgetting may often occur if the previously mastered material has been repeated but not reinforced. In such a case, we would anticipate that as a result of repeated nonreinforcement, the response in question (that is, the content memorized) would gradually become weaker. Moreover, the available evidence on punishment would

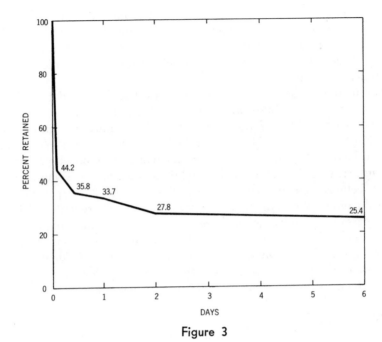

Figure 3

Ebbinghaus's retention for lists of nonsense syllables. Retention is measured by method of savings. (Adapted from R. S. Woodworth, Experimental Psychology. *New York: Henry Holt and Co., Inc., 1938. Data from Ebbinghaus, 1885.)*

lead us to expect that the individual's ability to repeat material that he had previously remembered may be impaired if he has had several experiences in which the performance of these responses has been followed by punishment. Note that in both of these examples, forgetting would occur despite the fact that material to be remembered had been practiced.

The disuse theory has other difficulties as well, for even though the amount of material we forget tends to increase as time passes, time itself does not necessarily *cause* forgetting. We may profitably consider an analogy: children tend to grow with the passage of time, but does this mean that time causes growth? We might more plausibly conclude that the underlying biochemical and genetic processes that control growth have an opportunity to produce their effects as time passes. A similar argument may be applied to forgetting. Forgetting is caused by the events that occur after the initial learning experience, not by the passage of time.

FORGETTING AND ORGANIZATION

While it is most common to think about forgetting as an almost universal occurrence following learning, some matters are more readily forgotten than others. One important determinant of forgetting is the degree of organization within the content to be remembered; material that is well structured and tightly organized will generally be recalled far more successfully than that which does not possess a meaningful structure. For example, in an experiment by Miller and Selfridge (1950) college students were read lists of words ranging in length from ten to fifty words each. Their job was to recall each list immediately after it was read. Some of the lists were completely unorganized; each of these unorganized lists simply consisted of a random collection of unrelated words. Other lists were highly organized, since they were taken directly from passages of written English. Between these two extremes were several lists that varied in the extent to which they approximated normal English text. The results of this experiment clearly indicated that accuracy of recall was directly related to the organization of the words within each list. That is, people found it much simpler to recall words organized in sentences than to recall an equal number of isolated words. Moreover, the more sentence-like the word list, the more readily it was recalled. An experiment based on this study is outlined in the laboratory manual of this series (Lane and Bem, 1965).

Other organizational factors facilitate recall. Bousfield (1953) constructed a list of sixty words drawn from four distinct categories: animals, names, vegetables, and professions. The words were read in a random sequence, following which the subjects attempted to recall (in order) as many words as they could. The results indicated that lists of thematically related words (as above) were more readily recalled than comparable lists that differed only in the fact that their constituent words did *not* have any particular thematic consistencies. Another important finding in this study was that thematically related words tended to be recalled in clustered sequences (dog, cat, lion, etc.) despite the fact that they had not been presented in this order. Even though they had been instructed to recall the words in their original order, the subjects apparently reorganized the lists into thematic groups of words and then recited them one after another during the recall test. This type of finding is consistent with the hypothesis that the process of memory is often an active "effort after meaning," not just a passive retention of what has been presented (this notion will be further amplified below).

The results of these and other related studies clearly indicate that human subjects are more successful in recalling organized rather than unorganized materials. It seems likely that this superiority in recall is based on the fact that one can often recall a mass of *organized* details by memorizing the underlying rule (or structure) that holds them together; in this way, the structure serves as a "shorthand" that can be expanded into the concrete details of the task at hand. This generalization seems to have direct implications for memory in our everyday lives. Consider the student who is studying a body of new material, perhaps on the French Revolution. His recall may be enhanced if he can succeed in imposing some structure and coherence on this material—that is, if he perceives and understands the interrelationships among the various events cited. In contrast, we would predict poorer recall if he simply attempts to remember isolated dates, names, and occurrences, without regard for the way in which these elemental units might be related.

ORGANIZATION AND CODING

Many of the techniques that people use to aid recall are related to the simple principle that organization facilitates memory. To help them remember the notes associated with lines in the treble clef (e, g, b, d, and f), children are taught the sentence "Every good boy does fine." The spaces of the clef (f, a, c, and e) may be even simpler to remember, since collectively they spell the word "face."

The type of technique in which the material to be remembered is "stored" in a modified form is often referred to as *coding;* our first example is shown diagrammatically in Figure 4. Here we can see that the

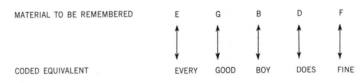

Figure 4

Example of coding in which each element to be remembered is stored in modified form.

number of elements to be retained is unchanged (that is, there is one word to be remembered for each note); and yet this type of coding will facilitate memory, since it is easier to recall the highly organized, familiar, and meaningful sentence, rather than the less meaningful set of isolated letters.

In another type of code that increases memory capacity, several of the items presented for memorizing are represented by a single item in the code. George Miller (1956) has reported an experiment in which the subject's task was to listen to a random series of zeros and ones which he was then to repeat in sequence. For example, he might be given the series 100111010101001010. Most people can successfully retain a series about nine digits long in this type of experiment. However, by recoding the original series following a system in which 000 = 0, 001 = 1, 010 = 2, 011 = 3, 100 = 4, etc. (see Figure 5), one of Miller's as-

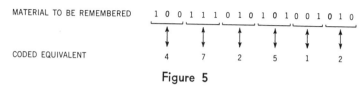

Figure 5

Example of coding in which three elements of material to be remembered are represented by one element in code.

sociates was able to recall strings over thirty digits in length. In this scheme, the subject first trained himself to respond to sets of three digits, which were represented in code by the numbers 0 through 7. If asked to remember the series 100111010100101001010, he would break the series into six groups. As shown in Figure 5, the first three digits (100) would be symbolized by the number 4, the next three (111) would be symbolized by the number 7, the next three (010) by the number 2, and the final three (triples) by the numbers 5, 1, and 2. Thus, by retaining only six numbers—4, 7, 2, 5, 1, and 2—and translating each of these back into its "zero-one" (or binary) equivalent, one could correctly recite an eighteen-digit list. In the actual experiment, this three-to-one coding ratio enabled Miller's subject to recall about thirty digits; other coding schemes in which each digit represented four or five elements in the original series of zeros and ones resulted in even better performance.

As noted above, this form of "many-to-one" coding facilitates performance partly because it reduces the number of things that must be remembered. In general, the ease with which we can symbolize the thing to be remembered (for example, the number of code units required for adequate symbolization) has a direct effect upon retention. Glanzer and Clark (1963) have reported an interesting experiment in which subjects were presented with a series of eight black or white geometric figures (diamond, circle, square, etc.) arranged in a horizontal array and projected on a screen for one-half a second. After viewing each array, subjects were given an answer sheet containing the geometric figures in the same arrangement in which they had appeared on the screen, and were instructed to write either a B (for black) or a W (for white) on each figure. As you might expect, it was much easier to recall the colors in some arrays than in others. For example, when all eight figures were black, 98 percent of the subjects could correctly recall the colors of all the figures; other arrays were more difficult, and could be correctly re-called by only 20 percent of the subjects.

What has all this to do with coding? Glanzer and Clark tested a second group of subjects and found that the arrays most readily re-called could be verbally described in a relatively few words (for ex-ample, "all black"). The arrays most difficult to recall, on the other hand, could be described only in rather lengthy terms by the average respondent in this second group (for example, "first, fourth, fifth, and eighth are black"). These data suggest that subjects in the recall task translated the stimulus input into its equivalent verbal form (or code) which they held in memory, and then used to guide their final written response. When the input stimulus could be coded (verbally symbol-ized) by a brief description consisting of only a few words, it was successfully recalled; when the stimulus required a lengthy verbal de-scription—that is, when it could not be efficiently coded—recall was less successful.

These data suggest that people with good memories may perhaps be blessed with relatively efficient coding systems for recalling the items that they wish to remember. They may be especially skillful in represent-ing the material to be recalled with relatively few verbal symbols; ideally, these verbal symbols should be organized into a meaningful structure. Devices of this sort provide a practical technique for improv-ing memory, and are probably responsible for the unusual feats of the so-called "memory expert."

ORGANIZATION AND MEMORY DISTORTION

Frederick Bartlett, an English psychologist, insistently pointed to the importance of organization and recoding in memory tasks (1932). He argued that we never simply receive and retain material that is to be recalled; instead, we reconstruct and schematize its essential details in an effort to make it "fit" with our own past experience. Bartlett thus contended that there is an "effort after meaning," an attempt to mold the material to the expectancies of the learner.

In support of this basic hypothesis, he cited several studies that used repeated reproduction. Subjects in these studies first read and then re-read an American Indian folk tale. Fifteen minutes later they were asked to reproduce the story, and subsequent reproductions were obtained still later. Because of their origin in a foreign culture, the stories had an unusual style and a supernatural content that contrasted with the stories most familiar to English-speaking peoples. Subsequent reproductions of the stories included many alterations that generally served to make the tales more congruent with our own cultural norms. There was, for ex-ample, a tendency to add new material designed to make better sense out of elements that most of us would regard as being strange and unconnected. In general, what seemed to be remembered was a central meaningful core which was preserved throughout each subject's several reproductions. On this basic framework, people tended to reconstruct the "original story" by filling in with more detailed material, some of which was recalled and some *invented*. Thus the individual's cultural expectancies, his personality, and his attitudes all contributed to what he "retained."

Bartlett contends that we rarely attempt to remember a given body of material in its full detail; instead, we schematize what is given to us. For example, we may frequently recall things that we have seen in the form of names or labels. Moreover, the names we choose in this process may play an important role in determining what we recall.

A famous experiment by Carmichael, Hogan, and Walter (1932) showed how the verbal labels associated with a set of ambiguous figures could influence subsequent reproductions of these stimuli. In this study, half the subjects were given one set of labels for the various experimental figures, and the other half were given a second set of labels. Figure 6 shows some of the original stimuli, the different labels associ-

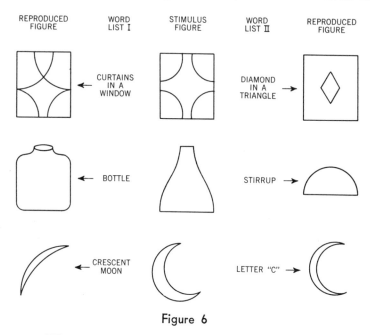

Figure 6

Effect of verbal labels on later reproductions of several ambiguous figures.

ated with each figure, and some of the subjects' reproductions of the stimuli. The results of this study, showing the impact of verbal labels upon memory, nicely paralleled Bartlett's view that we typically retain only a core schemata in memory (presumably a verbal label in this case), from which we attempt to "reconstruct" the original. A more recent study (Herman, Lawless, and Marshall, 1957) has suggested that even if subjects are *not* given verbal labels for the various stimuli in this type of study, they will implicitly "name" the figures on their own, and these labels too will influence their subsequent reproductions.

FORGETTING AND ACTIVE CHANGES IN THE MEMORY TRACE

We have previously referred critically to the statement that forgetting results from simple disuse. We noted that the passage of time did not, by itself, result in forgetting, but instead provided an opportunity for other factors to accomplish their effects. The experiments we have just discussed, showing how verbal labels may influence recall, provide a good example of the *systematic changes* in memory that may proceed as time passes. Note the contrast between a disuse theory, which posits a simple *fading* of the memory trace, and the results of these studies, which suggest that changes in the memory trace are not haphazard, but follow a definite, often meaningful, course.

Psychologists of the Gestalt school have long contended that memory traces are "active" in that they presumably evolve into simpler structures with the passage of time. The Gestalt view is most applicable to perceptual memories, for it holds that modifications of the memory trace tend to reduce the imbalances and perceptual stresses that characterized the original stimulus. For example, according to the law of *closure,* one often sees incomplete familiar figures as if they were whole; an incomplete circle with a small gap in one side will thus generate perceptual "stresses" that will sometimes lead people to perceive this figure as if it were complete. When a figure of this sort is retained in memory, according to the Gestalt view, even if it was accurately perceived at first, the memory trace will tend to change in the direction of completeness. Consequently, if we conduct recall tests at varying intervals after the initial presentation of such a stimulus, by having people draw the original figure as they remember it, the gap in the circle should gradually shrink, until we reach a stage where the circle is remembered as having been whole, with no uncompleted gaps. Although there is good evidence that memory traces undergo systematic changes as time passes, the Gestalt emphasis on *perceptual* forces as active agents in memory distortion has not been satisfactorily verified.[1]

---

[1] See, in this series, Walker and Weintraub on *Perception* (1966) for a fuller discussion of Gestalt theory.

MEMORY AND RESPONSE COMPETITION

One of the early and best-known experiments on memory (Jenkins and Dallenbach, 1924) clearly demonstrates the importance of the learner's activities after his initial exposure to the material he is to retain. In this study, two students at Cornell University learned lists of nonsense syllables and were tested for retention two, four, or eight hours later. The experiment was designed so that the students sometimes slept during the time that elapsed between their original learning of the lists and the subsequent test for retention. At other times, they were awake during this period and went on with their normal daily activities. While there was a certain amount of forgetting under both conditions, the students forgot less material while they slept than during waking hours. (See Figure 7.)

Experiments of this sort suggest that the sheer passage of time is less important as a determinant of memory than are the activities following the original learning experience. Psychologists speak of this phenomenon as *retroactive inhibition;* the main point here is that the activities in which we engage, subsequent to learning, often tend to interfere with or inhibit the recall of material memorized earlier.

A given activity will produce varying amounts of retroactive inhibition, depending upon its particular relationship to the originally learned material. From the considerable research on this matter, one suggested general conclusion is that, when tasks can be analyzed into stimulus-response sequences, retroactive inhibition is strikingly affected by the degree of similarity between the stimuli involved in the two tasks. For example, it has been repeatedly shown that when the stimuli are relatively unchanged from one task to the next, but the required responses are different, a considerable amount of retroactive inhibition will be produced. On the other hand, better retention will result if the stimuli of the two tasks are quite different. Suppose you have been studying French vocabulary using a flash card method in which you look at an English word (stimulus) and try to supply its French equivalent (response). Your recall of this material will be inhibited if you next turn to the study of Russian, using the same study technique and the same group of vocabulary words, for in this case the same English words (stimuli) appear in both lessons but you must learn two different responses to each—one French and one Russian. In contrast to the above sequence of study experiences, you would probably forget less of the French if you had subsequently studied something unrelated, such as biological definitions. Figures 8 and 9 show how we may diagrammatically represent these two tasks in terms of their stimulus and response components.

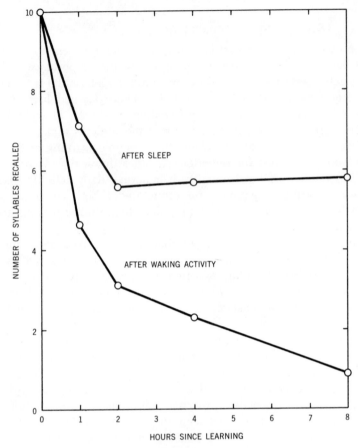

Figure 7

Effect on retention when sleep or waking activity follows initial learning. (Adapted from H. H. Kendler, Basic Psychology. New York: Appleton-Century-Crofts, 1963. Data from Jenkins and Dallenbach, 1924.)

Most psychologists feel that retroactive inhibition is a result of competition between responses. Thus, after learning our French lesson, the study of Russian may produce two important consequences. First, the Russian words may compete with the French and produce an "unlearning" effect; that is, the Russian words may *replace* the French as learned responses to the various English stimulus words. Second, even if the French responses have not been forgotten, when we test for recall there is likely to be some confusion and competition between the French and Russian; we may mistakenly answer with a Russian word when we are being tested on our French lesson.

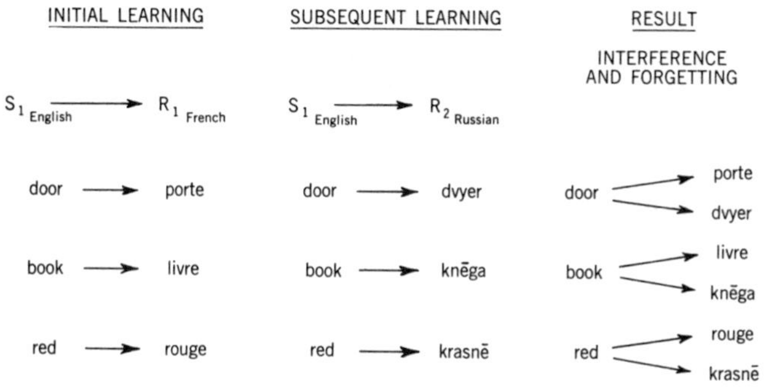

INITIAL LEARNING	SUBSEQUENT LEARNING	RESULT

Figure 8

A sequence that would produce marked retroactive inhibition due to similarity between stimuli in initial and subsequent learning tasks.

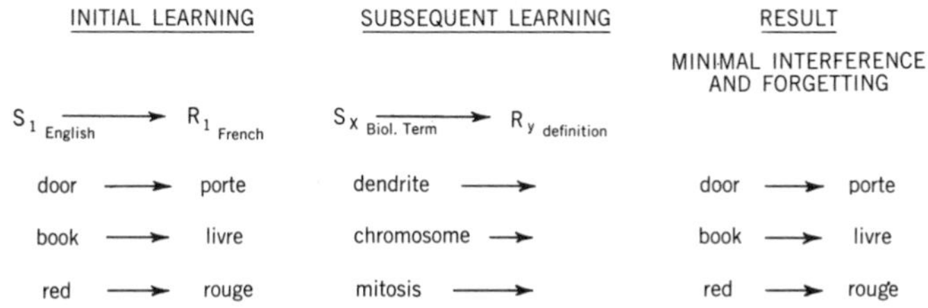

Figure 9

Sequence that would produce minimal retroactive inhibition because of dissimilarity between initial and subsequent learning tasks. (Adapted from J. Deese, Principles of Psychology. Boston: Allyn and Bacon, Inc., 1964.)

One of the best techniques for reducing retroactive inhibition is called *overlearning.* This involves continued practice at a given memory task, even after the learner has reached a level of errorless performance. The available research thus suggests that if the student in our hypothetical French lesson had practiced his vocabulary lesson beyond the point of initial mastery, his retention of this material would be much improved despite the potentially disrupting effects of a subsequent study session involving Russian vocabulary.

In studying retroactive inhibition we are concerned with the effects of subsequent activity on the retention of material learned in the past. *Proactive inhibition,* a related phenomenon, refers to the fact that some of the things learned in the past make it more difficult to remember things now being learned.

The importance of proactive inhibition was dramatically shown by

Underwood (1957), who pointed to the rapid decline in memory characteristic of Ebbinghaus's results, as contrasted with the slower rate of forgetting typically obtained in more recent studies. Since Ebbinghaus always carried out his work on the learning and retention of nonsense syllables with a very experienced subject, *himself,* his rapid forgetting of nonsense syllables recently learned might have been due to confusion with other lists he had learned.

To clinch his argument, Underwood designed an experiment in which the subjects learned varying numbers of nonsense syllable lists before being tested for retention of the last list they learned. His main purpose was to see if the amount recalled from this last list was affected by the number of lists that his subjects had learned in the past. His results showed clear evidence of proactive inhibition. In contrast to Ebbinghaus's practice, the study of memory is now carried out through the participation of relatively *inexperienced* subjects, who do not have to contend with the competing effects of previously learned lists of nonsense syllables and hence forget more slowly.

Underwood's results suggest that our ability to recall the things we have just learned may be drastically impaired if we have previously been forced to memorize large amounts of similar materials. While this conclusion holds for data discussed above, we must be careful in applying this rule. For example, it seems likely that a trained physician would be more successful in recalling the contents of an article dealing with tuberculosis than an engineer of equal intelligence, even though the physician would have read many more such articles in the past. How can this be reconciled with Underwood's findings? It seems most likely that Underwood's results are partly attributable to the fact that the successive materials learned in his studies were not related in any meaningful way. Each list, for example, typically contained a set of unrelated words or nonsense syllables, and there was no logical relationship between one list and the next. On the other hand, our hypothetical physician could immediately fit the material on tuberculosis within the framework of other information he had acquired on this topic and hence could more readily recall it. The engineer's lack of a medical background might make it difficult for him to organize the material and relate it to other information with which he was familiar; he would thus have more difficulty recalling it than the doctor would.

MOTIVATION AND MEMORY

In studying the cognitive processes of his patients, Sigmund Freud noted that they were often unable to recall anxiety-provoking events or events associated with fearful occurrences. He hypothesized that these memory lapses represented the operation of a mechanism he termed *repression,* through which anxiety-provoking materials were sometimes automatically "banished" from consciousness, despite the individual's conscious efforts to recall them. While we focus on the relationship between repression and *memory*, we should note that repression may also be applied to the individual's lack of awareness of the *motives* that guide him. Thus, according to Freud, we may employ repression both to prevent us from consciously recognizing some of the antisocial motives that underlie much of our everyday behavior, and to prevent conscious recall of unpleasant events.[2]

While contemporary psychologists generally accept the view that anxiety-provoking events are frequently difficult to recall, they are often critical of the relatively impressionistic data that are obtained in the course of clinical practice and have attempted to investigate the process of repression in the laboratory. Unfortunately, this has proven to be a complex matter; indeed, experimental studies of repression have often been criticized as being poorly designed, or naive regarding psychoanalytic theory.

Stagner (1931) conducted one of the early experiments in this area. In this study, a group of college students who had just returned from vacation wrote a description of one pleasant and one unpleasant incident that they had experienced. Below each description they then wrote their associations to the two incidents. Two weeks later, they were unexpectedly given copied versions of their descriptions and were asked to recall the associations that they had given previously. The results indicated that the average student could recall more associations to the pleasant incident than to the unpleasant incident. It should be noted, however, that experiments of this sort do not rule out the possibility that the obtained differences in recall might have been caused by rehearsal; that is, the students may have done more thinking and talking about the pleasant event than the unpleasant one, and consequently the obtained effects may be explainable in these simple terms, without involving a complex mechanism like repression. (In psychological experimentation, as in other scientific fields, the sophisticated investigator tries to be conservative in interpreting his findings. He attempts to explain a given set of results by turning to the most simple explanatory principle that proves sufficient; complex explanations are accepted only when the simple accounts prove inadequate.)

In another investigation, Zeller (1950) suggested that a successful demonstration of repression requires not only that the imposition of some threatening experience should produce forgetting of related memories, but that the removal of the threat should be accompanied by a *recovery* of the previously repressed materials. Following this line of thought, the

---

[2] In this series, see Blum, *Psychodynamics* (1966) for a more comprehensive discussion of Freud's views.

investigator arranged an experimental situation in which one group of students was subjected to a personal failure experience shortly after they had successfully mastered a list of nonsense syllables. In a subsequent test of recall, these subjects performed more poorly than a control group who had experienced success, rather than failure, following their initial learning experience. These results were attributed to repression, on the assumption that the nonsense syllables had become associated with failure (and anxiety) for the experimental group, and that this had caused the syllables to be forgotten. When these subjects were subsequently given an opportunity to succeed on the task that they had previously failed, and were then tested for retention, they showed improved recall of the nonsense syllables. To the extent that this experiment is relevant to the Freudian concept, these data suggest that repression may not be permanent, but may be reversed when the material to be remembered is no longer associated with negative effects.

Several memory experiments that may be related to repression have been concerned with the individual's ability to remember materials that conflict with his personal attitudes and beliefs. During the administration of Franklin D. Roosevelt, Edwards (1941) delivered a speech to a class of students; the speech included an equal number of statements favorable and unfavorable to the New Deal. In testing his students later, he found that most of the arguments that they remembered supported their preferred views regarding the New Deal; those who backed the New Deal remembered more favorable than unfavorable statements, while those who opposed it showed the reverse tendency. These results seem consistent with a repressive-like mechanism if we make the reasonable assumption that the students found it somewhat disturbing to learn that a respected professor held views diametrically opposed to their own personal beliefs.

THE ZEIGARNIK EFFECT

In investigating the impact of motivation upon memory, some investigators have postulated that, when actively working on a task, people develop "task tensions" that do not dissipate until they have completed the job at hand. If the task is not completed because of some interruption, this tension remains and the individual should, according to theory, continue to think about the uncompleted task and should be motivated to complete it, if given an opportunity.

In a classic test of this hypothesis, Zeigarnik (1927) had a group of subjects attempt a series of twenty different simple tasks, such as naming twelve cities beginning with the letter K, punching holes in a sheet of paper, molding an animal from clay, etc. On half of these tasks, the subjects were "accidentally" interrupted before completion, while they were permitted to finish the other half.

When the series was over, the subjects were asked to recall the names of as many tasks as they could. The results indicated that 80 percent of the subjects recalled more of the uncompleted than of the completed tasks—a finding now known as the *Zeigarnik effect*. As indicated above, this phenomenon is generally attributed to the presence of undissipated tensions associated with the interrupted tasks. A further finding that supports this interpretation is that subjects often returned spontaneously to the incomplete tasks when given an opportunity to do so.

At first glance, the Zeigarnik effect seems somewhat inconsistent with the concept of repression. If we assume that people prefer to complete the things they start, we might anticipate that they would repress their memory of tasks left incomplete. This argument gains still greater force if, for some reason, the subject interprets the experimenter's interruption as a sign that he has failed to complete a problem within its allotted time. How might this apparent conflict be resolved?

Two studies (Rosenzweig, 1943; Lewis and Franklin, 1944) suggest that the issue may hinge upon whether the subjects in the experiment are *task-oriented* or *self-oriented* (or *ego-involved*) toward their personal success in the experiment. To induce task orientation, subjects are led to believe that their main job is to help the experimenter standardize his procedures; to achieve ego-involvement, the experimenter's instructions suggest that the subject's performance will reflect his intellectual ability. If the standard interruption procedures are applied to subjects under task orientation, Zeigarnik's original result showing superior recall of incomplete tasks is generally obtained. When, however, the subjects are ego-involved, the interruptions are interpreted as failures, and subjects often show superior recall of the completed "successful" problems, presumably because they have repressed recall of the incomplete problems.

SUMMARY

1. Ebbinghaus inaugurated the scientific study of memory. He invented the nonsense syllable and the method of savings, which are techniques still widely used in memory research.

2. Forgetting does not proceed at a uniform rate. Immediately after learning, we are likely to forget rather rapidly; as time goes on, however, we forget at a slower rate.

3. Forgetting does not result from sheer passage of time. Instead, once we have memorized something, the amount that we subsequently forget is importantly affected by the things we do and learn after the original memorization session.

4. It is easier to remember highly organized material than unorganized material. Moreover, in trying to recall things, people will often *spontaneously* organize the material presented to them, even though they

have not been instructed to do so. In memory, then, we do not simply receive and retain information; instead, we typically restructure the material to be recalled in order to make it compatible with our previous experience.

5. In retroactive inhibition, things we learn will often interfere with our ability to recall other things learned in the past. Large amounts of retroactive inhibition will generally be produced when the stimuli involved in successive learning tasks are essentially unchanged but the required responses are different.

6. In proactive inhibition, some of the things we learned in the past may make it more difficult to remember the materials that we are currently attempting to memorize.

7. Clinical data suggest that people often find it difficult to remember anxiety-provoking incidents because of the mechanism of *repression*. Some laboratory studies also support this conclusion.

8. People often find it easier to remember tasks they have worked on but have not completed (due to interruption) than tasks that they have finished. This phenomenon is known as the *Zeigarnik effect;* it is generally attributed to "task tensions" that are assumed to remain active until the individual has completed the task at hand.

GOING BEYOND WHAT IS GIVEN   4

Learning often seems to be a relatively simple and straightforward process, if we limit our attention to the specific stimuli and responses directly involved in a given performance. If, for example, a child has been consistently reinforced for cooperative behavior in stimulus situations involving other children, it hardly seems surprising to find that ultimately he will behave cooperatively. However, we should not be misled by the apparent simplicity of his performance, for it is probably accompanied by a variety of related sequences that have not been explicitly taught. For example, the child may exhibit a *different form* of cooperation when interacting with a *new group* of acquaintances. In the words of Jerome Bruner, people frequently tend to "go beyond what is given." The knowledge that the learner acquires is *not* limited to the particular stimuli and responses that may have been involved in his original learning experience.

In anticipation of the material to come, let us note that in going beyond the given, two processes are involved. In the first, *stimulus generalization,* a given response can often be elicited by stimuli not explicitly linked with it through direct training in the past. In the second process, *response generalization,* the learner may repeat previously rewarded behaviors in various ways, and will not restrict himself to the precise movements that have previously been successful.

STIMULUS GENERALIZATION

A response associated with a given stimulus can usually be elicited by other stimuli, especially when these stimuli are reasonably similar to the stimulus involved in the original training. The fact that stimulus generalization occurs is often quite fortunate, for we are rarely exposed to precisely the same situation from one time to the next. Generalization permits us to show the steady effects of learning, despite the changing nature of the situations we encounter. The child who had learned to address his father as "daddy" can respond quite adequately even though his father may look slightly different because he is wearing a new suit or a new tie. This type of generalization, which is mainly based upon the physical similarity of the relevant stimuli (father-in-a-blue-suit versus father-in-a-brown-suit), may be referred to as *primary stimulus generalization.*

A second form of stimulus generalization, which is particularly important for an understanding of complex human behavior, is *mediated generalization.* This term is reserved for cases in which stimulus generalization occurs despite an absence of physical similarity between the training stimulus (the stimulus involved in the initial learning) and other stimuli capable of eliciting the response. A child who has learned to answer the question "Who wrote the Declaration of Independence?" will probably be quite capable of responding correctly even if we alter the specific words in which this question is phrased. Moreover, assuming that he can read, he will respond appropriately if the question is presented in written rather than spoken form. In both of these cases, although we have modified the question (stimulus) so that its constituent physical properties have all been radically changed, our young learner may well respond quite correctly without further training. Mediated generalization is quite common; indeed, we would hardly consider that the child had successfully mastered the original question-answer sequence if he was unable to respond appropriately to a variety of wordings and methods of presentation.

The examples of generalization given above represent rather complex situations quite unlike the laboratory settings that most psychologists prefer to deal with. Let us turn, therefore, to a relatively straightforward procedure in which both primary and mediated stimulus generalization may be demonstrated in a simple laboratory experiment.

Consider a situation in which a series of words is repeatedly presented, one at a time, on a screen. Assume that our subjects are instructed to press a response button as soon as each word appears. After our subjects have gone through this word list several times, we are ready to test for primary and mediated stimulus generalization. In this test we will present our subjects with another series of words—some drawn from our original list and some not previously used in the experiment. The subjects will be instructed to signal with the response button whenever they see a word drawn from the original word list.

Among the new items in our test list, we will make certain that some of the words look like words from the original list. We may conclude that our subjects' behavior is the result of primary stimulus generalization if, for example, the word "JOY" had initially been presented and our subjects respond positively to words like "BOY" or "TOY" or "JOT" (rather than to unrelated words like "BAT" or "SUN").

To test for mediated generalization, our test list would include several words that did not look or sound like those that had previously been shown but which were nevertheless meaningfully related to these words, perhaps as synonyms. If (as above) the word "JOY" had been among the original words, our subjects might, for example, show a strong tendency to respond when presented with the word "GLEE." If this were to occur regularly, we would conclude that our procedures had yielded evidence of *secondary* or *mediated generalization.*

While primary stimulus generalization seems readily understand-able—partly because of simple perceptual errors—mediated generaliza-tion is somewhat more complex. In attempting to develop an explanation of this phenomenon, let us start with the fact that your body is quite richly endowed with proprioceptors, which are essentially receptors that "feed back" signals concerning your present posture and recent move-ments. In short, these receptors are stimulated by the reactions and the present state of your body, rather than by the external stimuli that stimu-late your eyes and your ears. When a soldier snaps to attention, his proprioceptors signal that his posture is erect and muscles tensed. Simi-larly, when you react with fear following a narrowly averted automobile accident, your heart rate will usually be increased and you will doubt-less be aware of this because of the sensitive feedback from your pro-prioceptors. Psychologists believe that this form of feedback is produced by virtually every response we make, although the resulting pattern of stimulation is usually not so dramatic or intense as that which accom-panies fear.

Let us return now to our hypothetical experiment. Why do "JOY" and "GLEE" elicit similar reactions? If our experimental subject was familiar with English, we would assume that presentation of the word "JOY" automatically elicited a learned response, which some psychologists have referred to as a "meaning response." We shall elaborate this theory later on; for our present purposes it is sufficient to say that meaningful words produce responses in the listener or reader, even though these responses may often be impossible for the external observer to detect. These responses may, for example, consist of minimal changes in muscu-lar tone, or in an altered pattern of neural firing. For the typical English-speaking adult in our experiment, we may therefore assume that the "meaning response" (r_m) to the word "JOY" automatically produces a distinctive pattern of proprioceptive feedback or response-produced stimulus (s_m), as shown in Figure 10. If this analysis is correct, we can see that the effective stimulus for the button-pushing response in the

$$JOY \longrightarrow \left(r_{m_{joy}} \dashrightarrow s_{m_{joy}} \right)$$

Figure 10

Meaning response (r_m) *and its resultant pattern of proprioceptive feedback* (s_m) *following presentation of word "JOY."*

initial phase of our experiment may actually be the response-produced stimulus s_m, rather than the physical patterns of the letters J-O-Y as they appear on the screen. This is shown in the sequence starting with "JOY" in Figure 11. Now let us consider what will happen when a

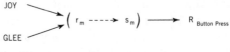

Figure 11

Mediated generalization based on similarity of meaning responses to words "JOY" and "GLEE."

synonym for "JOY"—"GLEE," for example—is presented during the test phase of the experiment. Since the two words have similar meanings, we assume that they elicit similar meaning responses in our subject, and ultimately result in rather similar patterns of proprioceptive feedback. This is shown in Figure 12 by the arrows that converge on r_m, the

STIMULUS GENERALIZATION   RESPONSE GENERALIZATION

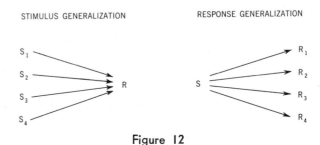

Figure 12

Diagrammatic representations of stimulus and response generalization.

meaning response common to both "JOY" and "GLEE," and its associated feedback pattern, s_m. Note further that if stimulus s_m is, in fact, the effective stimulus for the button-pushing response, we would expect this behavior to be exhibited whenever the stimulus pattern s_m is present, whether this pattern results from a chain of events starting with the original training stimulus "JOY," or is started by another word of similar meaning, such as "GLEE."

The importance of mediated generalization can readily be understood when we consider the variety of ways in which "the same" situation can occur. Think, for example, of the many ways in which a question may be phrased, or the many ways in which friendship can be expressed. The mechanism of mediated generalization permits us immediately to transfer well-practiced responses associated with one of these phrasings (or modes of expression) to others of equivalent meaning, without further training.

RESPONSE GENERALIZATION

When a given response has been associated with some stimulus, there is often a tendency for that stimulus to elicit other related responses. For example, Underwood and Hughes (1950) presented a series of adjectives to a group of subjects and later asked them to recall as many words as they could. The errors in recollection were striking, for there was a strong tendency to respond with synonyms, or words otherwise closely related to the adjectives on the original list. Results like this suggest that learning often strengthens the association between a given stimulus and a *cluster* of related responses. *Primary response generalization* is based upon the physical similarity of the two responses (that is, they may employ the same muscle groups in a similar pattern of action); *acquired response generalization* occurs between response elements that differ in their physical characteristics. In the Underwood and Hughes experiment discussed above, the errors in recollection mainly involved words meaningfully related to the correct responses, rather than words that looked or sounded like the correct answers.

Although the mechanisms underlying acquired response generalization are poorly understood at present, the importance of the phenomenon can hardly be overestimated. Consider a personality trait like cooperativeness. Many parents would like their children to act cooperatively, but recognize that it is impossible to teach *all* the different ways of being cooperative, in order to prepare the children for the infinite variety of situations they will encounter. Under these conditions, training is often based on the assumption that reinforcement of a given instance of cooperativeness (for example, sharing one's toys) will strengthen the entire family (or cluster) of cooperative acts (for example, helping in community projects, working effectively with associates on a job, etc.).

There is, however, some disagreement among psychologists concerning response generalization. Some psychologists assert that learning strengthens *specific* responses, not response *clusters*. In a famous experiment conducted by Guthrie and Horton (1946), cats were placed in a glass box from which they could not escape unless they activated a release mechanism—a pole set on a rocking base. Motion pictures were taken of the cats' behavior, which showed a remarkable degree of stereotypy from one trial to the next. For example, one cat learned to activate the mechanism by brushing the right side of his body against the pole; this same pattern remained remarkably stable throughout the experiment, even though the same results could have been achieved through a variety of responses. Despite this dramatic demonstration of response stereotyping, most psychologists believe that response generalization plays an important role in human and animal behavior, and several studies have now validated the phenomenon.

Figure 12 is designed to clarify the distinction between stimulus and response generalization. As shown, stimulus generalization refers to the fact that several stimuli may be *functionally equivalent;* all stimuli may elicit a response originally linked to only one member of the stimulus set. In response generalization, on the other hand, a stimulus associatively linked with a given response acquires the capacity to elicit other related responses.

The tendency to generalize from the explicitly "given" elements of a learning situation is an important and usually adaptive aspect of human behavior. In most situations it is primarily important that we correctly identify the category to which a stimulus belongs, and select our response from an appropriate response cluster: the precise identification of a specific stimulus from among others in the same category, or the selection of a specific response from among a closely related set, is often unimportant. However, in some circumstances, specificity is desirable, and it is necessary to overcome our generalizing tendencies. For example, a musician must learn to detect minor differences between musical notes on his score (stimuli); moreover, while performing, he must learn to *respond* with the exact note called for, rather than one that resembles it in some way. This type of learning requires extensive *discrimination training* based on the precise use of reinforcements. The learning situation must be constructed to insure that reinforcements are provided only for proper stimulus-response sequences. Thus, reinforcement should be withheld when the desired response occurs at an inappropriate time (for example, in response to a stimulus that closely resembles the "proper" stimulus). Similarly, reinforcement must be withheld after a response that merely approximates the desired behavior. (See Walker, *Conditioning and Instrumental Learning,* 1966, for further details on discrimination training.)

GENERALIZATION AND COGNITION

In many situations a given behavioral sequence can be performed either (a) by recalling the specific elements involved, or (b) by remembering the elements because of their position within some more general cognitive structure. Suppose you were asked to remember the number 58121519222629. This is a long number, and you would doubtless have trouble recalling it all if you were to proceed digit by digit. However, the task becomes much simpler if you notice that the overall series can be broken into the units 5-8-12-15-19-22-26-29, in which we start with the number 5 and add 3, then 4, then 3, then 4, etc. Note that we have categorized many distinct elements into a single simple rule. Such a rule would dramatically simplify the memory task, for we would then be faced with the less arduous job of recalling one rule, rather than a long string of digits (Katona, 1940).

Ideally, in mastering any new body of knowledge, it would be desirable if the material could be arranged according to the general principles, without the need for extensive recall of details. A mastery of geometry, for example, should not reside in the ability to remember a series of specific proofs, but should instead consist of a few generalized skills concerning the manner in which proofs are demonstrated. If these general skills are properly learned and applied, they should enable the student to produce a variety of specific proofs even though the constituent details have not been memorized.

The merits of this general approach can be seen in any mathematical formula. Consider the formula for calculating the distance traveled by an automobile: $D = rt$, where D represents distance, r is the rate of travel, and t is the amount of time the car has been moving. This simple formula is a general statement that conveys a great deal of specific information that would otherwise have to be laboriously memorized, or set down in a rather detailed and complicated table. Without the formula, we would be forced to remember an endless series of specifics if we wanted to know the distance traveled under a given set of circumstances. Thus, we would have to recall that at 45 miles an hour, a car will travel 90 miles in two hours, and that at 50 miles an hour it will travel 150 miles in three hours, and so on. It is clearly more efficient to forget the specifics and recall our general formula.

The mastery of a general formulation has another virtue: it enables us to deal successfully with new specific instances that we may not have previously encountered. Thus, the student will be capable of solving new "distance problems" not explicitly taught in class, for if he masters his general formula he is equipped to solve problems involving an endless variety of speeds and times.

CONCRETENESS
AND ABSTRACTION

In our previous discussion we have contrasted two approaches to learning and memory: (a) the specific approach, focusing primarily on all the detailed aspects of a given performance sequence, and (b) the general (or generic) approach, emphasizing the more inclusive categories within which a particular stimulus or response may be placed. The specific approach is often referred to as *concrete* because it stresses explicit details of the situation (the "givens" of an S-R sequence). The generic approach, in contrast, has often been termed *abstract*, because details of the situation are not emphasized and the individual seeks instead to abstract what he considers essential. Thus, in learning to solve a set of related algebra problems, he would largely ignore the particular wordings and quantities involved and retain instead the abstract association between the general class of problems and the appropriate mode of solution.

Unfortunately, at present only limited information is available concerning the factors that underlie development of the abstract approach. However, several studies have shown that people who have suffered brain injuries often show impaired abstracting ability. For example, they may find it difficult to note correctly the important general similarities between such discrete items as a car and a boat (both modes of transportation), and may instead focus on unessential concrete details in which the items being compared are *identical* (both cars and boats are made of metal). This form of concreteness may also be revealed in nonverbal tests that require the subject to sort a variety of objects into groups, whose members "belong together." Here the subject may be given such objects as a spoon, a knife, a candle, a hammer, some matches, a pipe, a ball, and so on. These objects can be grouped in many ways: by color, by the material from which they are constructed, by their uses, etc. After the subject has grouped the objects according to one system he may next be asked to group them according to some other system. Typically the brain-damaged person finds it more difficult to switch from one grouping to the next than does the normal person. It is as if the brain damage makes it more difficult for the individual to recognize that *many* abstract schemes may be employed in grouping the stimuli. Thus, if he finds color differences most striking and hence performs his initial grouping based on this principle, he may subsequently find it difficult to shift to another grouping (object uses, perhaps) that would require him to place objects of different colors into the same category. In this example, we may infer that the concrete color details have dominated our subject's sorting behavior and have prevented him from grouping the objects in other possible arrangements.

Some studies performed with these sorting techniques have suggested that abstract performance not only is impaired by brain damage, but is also deficient among schizophrenics, and is typically quite limited in children. While some observers have suggested that the schizophrenic's concreteness represents a regression to the childish behavior of the youngster, this conclusion may be unwarranted, for the schizophrenic's performance often seems qualitatively unlike that of the child.

SUMMARY

1. Upon learning a given stimulus-response sequence, the individual usually "goes beyond what is given"; that is, he may treat the specific stimulus and response elements of a single association as if they represented rather *general categories*. Two processes are involved here: *stimulus generalization* and *response generalization*.

2. In stimulus generalization, a response associated with a given stimulus through direct training may also be associatively linked with *other* stimuli as a further consequence of this training. Usually, this form of generalization is strongest when we consider stimuli closely related to one another. For example, a child who has learned to label a circular design (stimulus) as a "circle" (response) will also be likely to use this term in referring to "near-circular" shapes, such as the oval. In a case like this, where the generalization is based on physical similarity between the relevant stimuli, the process may be termed *primary stimulus generalization*. *Mediated generalization* is based on the *learned equivalence* of stimulus elements that are physically unrelated.

3. In response generalization, learning generally strengthens a *cluster* of related responses, rather than just *one*. Here we may distinguish between (a) *primary response generalization*, where the responses are physically related in the sense that they involve similar muscle groups, and (b) *acquired response generalization*, which involves response elements that may differ in their physical characteristics.

4. By "going beyond what is given," the learner essentially emphasizes the general structure of the task he is learning, and he is somewhat less involved with recalling the specific elements that comprise the situation. This approach aids memory, for it is usually simpler to recall a general structure rather than a series of isolated stimulus and response elements. Moreover, the general approach often enables the learner to deal successfully with specific instances not previously encountered.

5. People who have suffered brain damage often find it difficult to adopt the general (or abstract) approach. Instead, their cognitive processes may show a concrete emphasis upon specific details in problem solving, which may interfere with effective performance.

Consider the problem that a child faces as he learns to use the word "dog." For our present purposes, this word may be considered a label or name that he must learn to apply appropriately. The immediate problem that he faces is this: Which of the many things and objects around him may he properly label as dogs? Notice that we expect him to attach this *identical label* ("dog") to a variety of rather *individualized* animals (some short, some tall; some brown, some spotted; some long-haired, some short-haired). Moreover, once the word has been completely mastered, we expect that he will be able to apply it correctly to new animals that may differ noticeably from those he has seen before. For example, if we show him an exotic breed with rather unique markings, we expect that our knowledgeable child will correctly identify it as a dog, even though he has never seen an animal quite like it before. This example illustrates some of the features that characterize *concept formation.*

Perhaps the most basic aspect of concept formation is that it involves a single response (for example, a single label or action) that is to be associated with a variety of distinguishable stimuli (for example, objects or events).

In a sense, our ability to classify the world into such conceptual *categories* as dogs, fires, friends, justice, etc., is a considerable advantage, for it often enables us to apply past reactions to new things and events that we encounter every day. It may be argued, for example, that we never encounter exactly the same event twice. The fact that a variety of objects may properly be given the same label (dog) will thus enable us to make an appropriate adjustment (cautious friendliness perhaps) on our first encounter with a given dog. This type of transfer can best be understood if we recall our earlier comments concerning mediating responses and proprioceptive (self-produced) stimulation. In the present case (see Figure 13), we have assumed that, in the past, the overt response of cautious friendliness has been associated with animals that overtly or implicitly elicited the mediating label (r_m) "dog" and its resulting feedback pattern ($s_{m_{dog}}$). When a strange animal (dog_x) elicits the familiar label, the resulting feedback ($s_{m_{dog}}$) leads to the usual overt behavior, despite the absence of any previous contact with the dog in question. We should, of course, hasten to add that an overly broad conceptual system for categorization may often be maladaptive; failure to differenti-

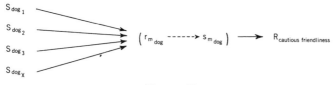

Figure 13

Response transfer due to presence of common mediating label (r_m) *elicited by variety of dogs.*

ate between a diseased dog and run-of-the-mill dogs may have unfortunate consequences.

Psychologists have identified several types of concepts, each based on a different labelling system. The *conjunctive concept* is well exemplified by the "dog" example above. In concepts of this sort, the labelling rule requires that all instances (or exemplars) of the concept must have a *single common attribute* or *several common attributes*. The important thing to remember is that, in at least one way and perhaps several ways, all exemplars of the concept are alike. Thus, in learning the concept "dog," the main problem is to recognize features *essential* in determining the "dogginess" of the animal before us (number of legs, tail, fur, and so on) and to ignore irrelevant features (hair color, length of tail).

In a *disjunctive concept*, the constituent exemplars do not all share any single characteristic or group of characteristics. Instead, there may be several *alternative* characteristics—any one of which will justify the inclusion of a given exemplar within the concept. For example, consider the concept of a "strike" in baseball. A pitch may be classified as a strike if it exhibits any one of the following characteristics: (a) a pitch that crosses home plate between the batter's shoulders and his knees, (b) a pitch that results in a foul ball, or (c) a pitch on which the batter swings and misses. Psychologists have only recently begun to investigate the acquisition of disjunctive concepts. However, the little research currently available suggests that these concepts are difficult to learn. Subjects often act as if they expected that the concept to be learned was organized conjunctively (rather than disjunctively), even though they are given no special reason to assume this. It is as if people generally expect that when different exemplars are given the same label, they must have some *common* underlying characteristic(s), and thus they find it difficult to accept the notion that two exemplars may both belong in the same category but for different reasons. For example, if we hear of two different cough medicines categorized as *effective remedies,* we ask what common features of these medicines explain their similarity, rather than assuming that the medicines may produce similar effects for different reasons.

The last type of concept that we will discuss is the *relational* concept.

Here, a single category may include quite diverse exemplars. Indeed, the exemplars are not grouped together because they share any particular feature (or features). Instead, the crucial factor is that each exemplar within the category shows some characteristic relationship. For example, in classifying two-digit numbers, we may employ a relationally defined rule that would include in a single category all cases in which the first digit was greater than the second. Such a category would include numbers like 32, 51, 63, etc., because each of these exemplars exhibits the crucial (defining) relationship among its constituent digits. To date, there has been very little research on the acquisition or utilization of relational concepts.

Most research on concept formation has been concerned with the process in which *conjunctive* concepts are learned and applied. One of the best-known studies in this area was conducted by Clark Hull. In Hull's experiment (1920), subjects were presented with twelve decks of cards, each card containing several Chinese symbols. The subject's task was to learn the nonsense syllable to be associated with each card. Since the same set of syllables served as responses as the subject progressed from one deck of cards to the next, each response (label) eventually came to be associated with several cards (stimuli). Moreover, although Hull's subjects were not told in advance, each card contained a crucial element consistently associated with one particular response. For example, all cards that contained a check-like design were to be called "oo" regardless of the remaining content of the card and regardless of the deck in which the card appeared. Similarly, the presence of a "P-shaped" structure consistently signified that the card was an exemplar of the "na" concept. Hull observed that, with practice, his subjects were able to learn the various concepts in the deck; that is, *they could correctly label new instances of the concept when they were first presented.* One interesting and surprising observation was that some of Hull's subjects who had successfully learned to apply the concept labels were nevertheless unable to verbalize the cues to which they were responding. These subjects could apparently behave in accord with the labelling rules that the experiment required, and yet they were seemingly unaware of just how they went about doing this.

Following Hull's lead, experiments in concept formation have typically employed complex stimuli, each containing several irrelevant cues and some crucial (or relevant) cue that could be used to label properly each exemplar. The stimuli might thus be wooden blocks varying in shape (round versus square), color (red versus green), and size (large versus small). The subject's task would be to place each block in one of the two categories, which might be arbitrarily labelled with such nonsense syllables as DAK and VEC. The experimental session might proceed in the following manner: The different blocks (stimuli) would be presented one at a time, and the subject would attempt to label each one appropriately. Following each trial, the subject would be informed if his response was "right" or "wrong." The experimenter might reinforce the subject when his responses conformed to some preselected conjunctive rule—such as, green stimuli = DAK; all others = VEC.

CONTINUITY VERSUS DISCONTINUITY

Does concept learning represent a continuous or a discontinuous process? Does the learner *gradually* come to recognize that color, for example, is the *revelant* cue that determines the correct categorization of each stimulus? Or, on the other hand, is concept learning discontinuous? Perhaps the subject actively tests a series of hypotheses ("maybe all the tall ones are VEC's") in attempting to discover the correct categorization rule, and *only learns about the correctness or incorrectness of the hypothesis he is testing at any given time.*

The *discontinuity* approach suggests that if color were the relevant dimension in a concept-formation task, this fact would have virtually no impact upon the learner during trials in which he was "trying out" other hypotheses (shape, for example). According to the continuity hypothesis, however, even if the learner was focusing his attention on the wrong hypothesis, he would be gradually building up a tendency to respond in accordance with the crucial dimension. For example, according to the continuity theory, if our subject labels a *round green* block as a DAK (because he thinks shape is crucial), and is told that he is "right," this sequence of events should simultaneously strengthen his tendency to apply the DAK label (a) to subsequent round blocks and (b) to subsequent green blocks. If color is in fact the correct basis for labelling, our subject will eventually come to ignore the shape of the blocks in making his responses, since this cue would not lead to consistent success. As noted above, however, the continuity theory suggests that *throughout* the series of learning trials our subject will have *gradually* and *automatically* built up the association between the green stimuli and the DAK response, even though he may have been focusing on other, irrelevant dimensions during the initial steps of learning.

Although there is no complete agreement, recent evidence suggests that the discontinuity model may be more appropriate as a description of the concept-formation process in college students. On the other hand, several experiments suggest that the continuity approach may present a more faithful account of concept formation in animals and in children of average intelligence. What is the evidence for these assertions? Some investigators have studied the behavior of their subjects *before* they had fully mastered the concepts they were to learn. For example, many studies assume that a subject has completely learned a concept if he succeeds in responding correctly to ten successive stimuli. If concept learning is a continuous process, we should find that our subject's performance shows a steady improvement in the trials prior to his errorless run, as the crucial cue becomes more and more potent in guiding his response. On the other hand, if concept learning is discontinuous, we would expect that the subjects would perform at a chance level on trials preceding their discovery of the correct solution, while they are presumably testing out incorrect hypotheses. However, when the correct hypothesis occurs to the learner, he should, according to the discontinuity view, shift *abruptly* from chance performance to his final errorless level of performance. These hypothetical performance curves are shown in Figure 14, which shows the trends predicted by the two theories in the trials preceding complete mastery of the task.

In a study of concept attainment in elementary and junior high school children, Osler and Fivel (1961a) examined the ten trials just preceding each child's final errorless run and then classified their subjects as gradual or sudden learners, depending upon the number of correct responses achieved in this pre-solution series. Their results indicated that *bright* children (with IQ's above 110) were most likely to be sudden learners,

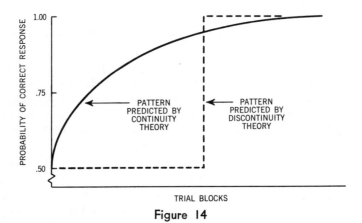

Figure 14

Performance curves in concept-formation task as predicted by continuity and discontinuity theories.

in that they showed relatively poor performance in the trials just preceding solution, while the *average* youngsters were less likely to learn suddenly. These data suggest that the bright youngster may solve concept-formation tasks by employing successive hypotheses, as outlined in the discontinuity theory, while the average child may rely on simple associative learning, as stressed by the continuity approach.

A subsequent study by Osler and Trautman (1961b) provides additional support for this conclusion. In this experiment, some children were presented with a rather simple concept-formation task in which they were to choose between two cards displaying different numbers of circles. One card of each pair had two black circles on it randomly placed, while the other card had either one, three, four, or five circles. The children could earn marbles, which could later be exchanged for a prize, by consistently choosing the card with the two circles. A second group of children was presented with a similar but somewhat more complex task in which they were to choose between two cards with pictures (rather than circles). Each picture contained between one and five common objects, each presented in a variety of sizes and colors. Once again, one card in each pair depicted the "two" concept (included two objects), and the children were reinforced for choosing this card—whether it contained two red cars, two walking boys, or any other group of two objects. Notice that in the simple task used with the first group, the stimulus cards differed from one another in only a few ways. The main differences between the stimuli involved the number of circles (the crucial cue) and the specific positioning of the circles. In the complex task, on the other hand, the stimulus cards differed in the number of objects depicted, in the specific objects shown, in color, size, and positioning on the card, and in several other ways. If, as suggested above, a bright child generally approaches concept-formation tasks in the manner assumed by the discontinuity approach, he would successively try out each of the available possibilities, and we would expect him to learn the simple task rather quickly, since there would be relatively few incorrect alternatives to eliminate before he recognized that the number of circles on each card was crucial. In contrast, it should take a bright child considerably longer to learn the complex task, since he might try many reasonable alternatives before finding the correct solution. These results were, in fact, obtained among the bright children, for the data clearly showed that they solved the simple task in fewer trials than the complex task.

The children of average intelligence learned the simple and complex concepts in about the same time. This result is consistent with the view that average children learn less by testing hypotheses than by steadily developing stimulus-response associations. For these children, then, regardless of the number of cues in the stimuli, there seemed to be a continuous development of association between the "twoness" concept and the subject's choice of response.

As you might expect from the results obtained with bright children, the available evidence suggests that college students typically solve concept-attainment tasks by the discontinuity approach. For example, Bower and Trabasso (1963) have examined the performance of students in a concept-formation task just prior to the achievement of solution. Their results clearly indicate that these subjects learn quite *suddenly* (presumably when they discover the correct hypothesis), because the data suggest that in the trials preceding solution, the subjects have been performing at about a chance level of performance and are right about as often as they would be through blind guessing. It seems reasonable to infer that they have been trying out one or more of the incorrect hypotheses before switching to the correct one.

A second line of evidence in support of the discontinuity notion, as it applies to college students, comes from studies in which the subjects first learn to respond to one aspect of the stimuli (color, let us say) and then find that, without warning, the task has been switched, so that shape is now the relevant aspect. In conducting this type of experiment, it is possible to arrange the stimuli so that, for example, most of the striped stimuli are *square*, and most of the unstriped ones are *round*. Under these conditions, if concept learning were *continuous*, we would expect that subjects would find it relatively easy to adapt to a new performance rule in which square stimuli were to be placed in the same category that had previously been used for the striped stimuli. Thus, Figure 15 shows that

STIMULI IN THE DAK CATEGORY   STIMULI IN THE VEC CATEGORY

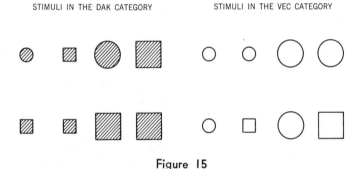

Figure 15

Stimuli for experimental test of continuity versus discontinuity theories of concept formation. Note that most striped stimuli are square, while unstriped ones are round.

in applying a striped-unstriped discrimination on the first concept (striped stimuli = DAK, unstriped stimuli = VEC), our subject has simultaneously (and inadvertently) been employing a round versus square discrimination on 75 percent of the stimuli. This should, according to continuity theory, facilitate subsequent concept learning based on the principle that square = DAK. Although the experimental details were somewhat different from those described above, a study of this general type has been conducted with college students (Gormezano and Grant, 1958); and contrary to the "continuity" prediction, the results unequivocally indicate that speed in learning a second categorization is unaffected by the extent to which this new grouping agrees with the initial learned conceptual rule. These results, then, support the discontinuity assumption that college students concentrate on one hypothesis at a time. While learning the first conceptual rule (striped versus unstriped stimuli in the above example), they fail to notice that utilization of other cues (shape) would lead to near-perfect performance. At any rate, their speed in mastering the second concept does not depend on the amount of "overlap" between the first and second concepts.

REVERSAL AND NONREVERSAL SHIFTS

The study of conceptual shifts has yielded still another interesting finding. Consider a situation in which the initial conceptual rule has been: all green objects = DAK; all red objects = VEC. After he masters this concept, we may now attempt to teach our subject a new conceptual rule. We may employ two basic types of conceptual changes. In one, termed a *reversal* (or *intradimensional*) *shift*, we simply reverse the labelling scheme without telling our subjects; that is, while color may still be the revelant dimension, according to our new rule all green stimuli = VEC (rather than DAK), and all red stimuli = DAK (not VEC). In a *nonreversal (or extradimensional) shift*, a dimension previously *irrelevant* would become *relevant*. For example, after learning to respond to color, subjects might now be required to learn a shape concept (square = DAK, round = VEC).

Normal adults find reversal shifts much simpler than nonreversal shifts (Kendler and D'Amato, 1955). This may seem surprising to you, since, as the name implies, a reversal shift requires a *complete change* in associations (for example, green stimuli now equal VEC, not DAK), while some of the stimuli maintain their original labels in a nonreversal shift. Thus, in the above example of a nonreversal shift, a green square previously labelled DAK because of its color, might because of its shape continue to receive the DAK label *after* the shift. The difficulty in learning nonreversal shifts is generally attributed to the fact that they require the subject to start "attending" to a dimension previously irrelevant. In learning a reversal shift, on the other hand, the initially relevant stimulus retains its importance and the subject's only problem is to relearn his labels. While the color cue may still be important, he must learn that the stimuli that used to be DAK are now VEC.

In contrast to the results obtained with normal adults, reversal shifts are more difficult than nonreversals for lower animals (Brookshire, Warren, and Ball, 1961). This difference between the performance of human adults on the one hand, and animals on the other, is thought to reflect differences in the processes involved in their conceptual learning. Adults are thought to respond primarily to the mediating verbal cues that they produce as they "attend to" (focus on) the relevant cue in each stimulus. For example, having discovered color as the relevant cue, the adult may respond to the implicit verbal label "green" with the appropriate overt response (DAK). Note that this same implicit label would be helpful in learning a subsequent reversal shift, since color would still be the relevant cue. In nonreversal shifts, on the other hand, the subject must discover anew which aspect of the stimulus (shape, for example) constitutes the relevant cue. Animals, having less symbolic facility than humans, are thought to respond directly to the external stimulus, rather than to some mediating verbal response. As a result, they find the reversal shift to be particularly difficult, since it requires them to extinguish an old habit *completely* and replace it with a new one.

The reasoning presented above suggests that children—who are less skilled in verbal facility than adults—should respond to shift problems more in the manner of the lower animals; reversal shifts should be more difficult for them than nonreversals (in contrast to the typical finding obtained with adults). The available evidence tends to support this view (Kendler and Kendler, 1959). Moreover, it has also been demonstrated (Kendler, 1964) that the child's ability to master reversal shifts may be significantly enhanced if he is given specific training in verbally describing the relevant aspects of the stimuli that constitute his task. In this study the children were to choose between two stimuli that varied in shape (square versus round) and color (black versus white). If they chose the correct stimulus, they were reinforced with a marble. Some children were given verbalization training by having them precede each of their choices with the sentence "The black is the winner and the white is the loser" (assuming that color was the relevant dimension). Other children were presented with a similar concept-formation task but were given no special instructions about verbalizing the cues to which they were responding. After all the children had mastered this initial task, they were presented with a second task, with no ostensible break in the procedure. The children's performance in this second task indicated that the verbalization training had facilitated the ease with which a reversal shift could be mastered. While this study involved the use of overt verbalizations on the part of the children, the adult's striking success in solving reversal shifts is probably related to the use of similar verbal mechanisms at a covert level.

STRATEGIES IN CONCEPT ATTAINMENT

In addition to studying the sheer speed with which concepts may be attained under various experimental conditions, psychologists have recently become interested in what has been termed the "strategy" of the concept learner. By strategy, we mean the overall manner in which the individual learner develops his hypotheses during concept formation. Consider the problem faced by a clinical neurologist seeking to discover areas of the brain essential for speech. In the course of his daily practice, he encounters many cases suffering from aphasia (impairment of speech). These cases do not show *identical* patterns of brain damage, and our neurologist is thus faced with the problem of discovering the "crucial" areas that, when damaged, lead to aphasia. How shall he proceed?

Suppose that the first aphasic he encounters shows extensive brain damage encompassing areas I through VI. One type of strategy often employed by college students when faced with a laboratory analogue of this problem may be termed a *wholist approach*. In our present example, this would take the form of initially adopting the hypothesis that all six of the damaged areas are essential to speech. So long as our neurologist continued to meet aphasics who showed damage in all six of these areas, he would maintain his initial hypothesis. Suppose, however, he were to examine one aphasic—or better yet, several aphasics—who showed damage in areas I, II, III, and VIII. A strict follower of the wholistic approach would then alter his hypothesis in order to account for features that the old hypothesis and the present instance(s) have in common. The new hypothesis would assert that aphasia results from damage to areas I, II, and III.

By adopting this approach, our neurologist will generate hypotheses that become increasingly "focused." He may, for example, continue to hypothesize that areas I, II, and III are all essential for the maintenance of normal speech, until he encounters an aphasic patient (or group of patients) who fails to show damage in all three of these areas. If he were to examine an aphasic who did *not* show damage in area II, the neurologist might focus his hypothesis still further to the assertion that only areas I and III were essential to speech. This is a slow and steady strategy, and one of its main virtues is the relative ease with which it can be executed. It is particularly undemanding in its memory requirements, for the learner need only recall his most recent hypothesis (in the present example, the neurologist's hypothesis is always a summary of features common to *all* the aphasics he has thus far encountered).

Scanning strategies present an interesting contrast to the wholist approach. A neurologist who followed a scanning approach would, essentially, "bet" on some area (or areas) as being crucial for speech. For example, if his initial aphasic patients showed damage in areas I through VI, our scanner might hypothesize (largely on the basis of a "hunch") that aphasia was produced by damage to areas I, IV, and VI, and that areas II, III, and V were irrelevant. If this hypothesis conflicted with his subsequent experience, it would, of course, be changed. Ideally, the new hypothesis would be consistent with all the instances previously seen. However, in reformulating his hypothesis our scanner (or partist) must rely heavily upon his memory, for the partist's hypothesis is *not* an up-to-date summary of features consistently associated with aphasia. As a result, when the partist is forced to revamp his hypothesis, he must attempt to recall all the individual aphasics he has previously encountered. Perhaps as a result of the heavy reliance on memory, this type of approach tends to be particularly inefficient if the learner is placed under time pressure. Under these conditions, laboratory studies suggest that the partist is often unable to execute successfully the rather complex cognitive activities that his strategy calls for. The more mechanical wholist approach, on the other hand, is less markedly affected by such forms of cognitive stress (Bruner, Goodnow, and Austin, 1962).

These two idealized strategies are seldom consciously and deliberately followed to the last detail, but people rather consistently act in general accord with one or the other of these approaches. They will tend to adopt a similar approach on a variety of concept-formation tasks. Moreover, the wholist strategy is more widely employed than the partist when bright college students are faced with the type of "neutral" concept-formation materials typically employed in the laboratory (for example, designs that vary in size, shape, color, etc.). However, in tasks of this sort, it is unlikely that the learner will enter the situation with strong biases and expectations based on previous experience. If we were to present our learner with complete descriptions of several hypothetical people—some of whom were known to be excellent salesmen—and his task was to learn the essential characteristics of this group, such "compelling" and "reasonable" attributes as intelligence or friendliness or physical appearance might be adopted as tentative hypotheses in the manner of the partist, even before such undramatic possibilities as place of birth or number of siblings had been systematically eliminated from consideration through the cautious focusing approach. In short, when the learner is presented with familiar meaningful materials, problem solving is likely to start with hypotheses that have previously been reasonable and useful, rather than with the more neutral and uncommitted wholistic strategy.

SUMMARY

1. Through concept formation, the individual learns to apply a single label to a variety of distinct but related instances (or exemplars). For example, when a child has successfully mastered the concept "dog," he will have learned to apply this same label to a variety of clearly distinguishable animals. He will, moreover, be capable of applying the appropriate label to dogs he has not previously encountered.

2. There are three main types of concepts. (a) In a *conjunctive concept* the different instances (or exemplars) of the concept must all share one or more common attributes. (b) In a *disjunctive concept* the different exemplars need not share any common characteristic; instead, they may be included in the same concept for one of several reasons (for example, a strike in baseball may be either a case in which the batter missed the

ball completely or it may be a "called" strike). (c) In a *relational concept*, the different exemplars are placed in the same class because they all show some particular relationship among their constituent attributes. For example, social interactions between pairs of siblings may be classed as symmetric if the interacting children respond similarly to one another, whether they are friendly, unfriendly, or withdrawn.

3. There is some controversy about the way in which conjunctive concepts are learned. One school of thought holds that, through reinforcement, people gradually and automatically come to associate the correct label with the various exemplars that belong within the same concept; this has been termed the *continuity theory*. In contrast, the *discontinuity approach* is based on the assumption that concepts are learned rather abruptly, as the individual tries out one hypothesis after another in an attempt to learn the correct labelling rule. Present evidence suggests that the continuity approach may provide an accurate characterization of concept formation in young children of average intelligence and in animals. On the other hand, gifted children and college students seem to learn concepts in accordance with the discontinuity approach.

4. Two rather distinct approaches (or strategies) have been identified in concept formation. In the *wholist approach* the learner starts with the most general hypothesis (or rule) for labelling the exemplars consistent with his experience, and then gradually and systematically narrows his hypothesis as he views more and more exemplars. On the other hand, in the *scanning* (or partist) approach the learner follows his hunches and successively attempts to select the correct labelling rule without proceeding in the systematic and increasingly focused manner that characterizes the wholist approach.

The study of language presents us with one of the most important and complex problems of contemporary psychology. Although language phenomena have also been of major concern to scholars in such diverse disciplines as philosophy, linguistics, speech, and anthropology, we shall concentrate primarily in this chapter upon the contributions of the psychologist and will review some of his approaches to studying language behavior.

B. F. SKINNER

B. F. Skinner (1957) has attempted to explain man's verbal behavior by means of concepts originally developed in the study of animal behavior. He stresses the extent to which verbal behavior can be effectively controlled through judicious use of *reinforcements* and *discriminative stimuli*. Skinner's approach can perhaps best be understood if we first review the meaning of these concepts (in this series, see Walker, *Conditioning and Instrumental Learning*, for a more complete review).

Responses that are reinforced (result in "positive" consequences) will tend to be repeated in the future. Thus, in a very simple case, a rat may be deprived of food and placed in an experimental chamber that contains a lever connected to a food-delivery mechanism. If the apparatus is arranged so that bar pressing results in the delivery of food pellets, the bar-pressing responses will tend to occur with increasing frequency. Conversely, if bar pressing does not produce reinforcement, it will not gain in strength and may indeed appear with decreased frequency in the future (extinction).

Many experiments at least suggestively related to the bar-pressing example demonstrate the influence of *social* reinforcements upon verbal behavior. In one experiment (Cohen, Kalish, Thruston, and Cohen, 1954), subjects were presented with a series of cards on which there appeared six personal pronouns ("I," "he," "she," "we," "they," "you") plus a verb; the same pronouns appeared on each card, although the verb was changed from one card to the next. Subjects were instructed to compose a sentence for each card by using one of the pronouns and the verb. The experimenters' main interest was in increasing the number of sentences that included the pronouns "I" or "we"; consequently, the experimenters reinforced the use of these pronouns by saying "good" whenever one was used in a sentence. Through this simple procedure, it was possible to "control" partially the subjects' verbal behaviors, for the results indicated that the reinforced pronouns ("I" and "we") were used with increasing frequency. Studies like this suggest that verbal responses may be strengthened through the operation of verbal reinforcements ("good"). However, in contrast to the case of the rat, a fair amount of evidence suggests that human behavior in this type of experiment may be largely under the control of conscious plans and hypotheses, and may not automatically reflect the operation of reinforcements (see p. 12; also Spielberger, 1962, for a more complete discussion of this issue).

Skinner uses the concept of the *discriminative stimulus* to account for the fact that, through appropriate training, a hungry rat can be taught to barpress *only under certain conditions* and not indiscriminately. For example, if bar pressing results in food pellets while a signal light is on (and not when it is off), the rat will soon learn this discrimination; he will engage in bar pressing when the light is on and refrain from this behavior when it is off. A similar process seems to occur in language behavior. A child can be trained so that he will say "thank you" only on certain occasions. As with the rat, discrimination training is accomplished by reinforcing the response when it occurs under appropriate circumstances (for example, when the child has just been given a candy bar) and withholding reinforcement if the response occurs when it is inappropriate.

If, as Skinner asserts, language can be adequately explained through an application of the same laws that apply to other forms of behavior, we might well ask if verbal behavior has any unique characteristics. Skinner feels that there is indeed one distinguishing hallmark: verbal behavior does not operate directly upon the environment to produce reinforcements, as the rat does when he presses the bar in his experimental chamber. Instead, verbal behavior most typically leads to reinforcement through an indirect medium involving the actions of others. For example, when eating dinner I may be faced with the problem of getting cream for my coffee. I can obtain this goal quite directly through the nonverbal act of reaching; or alternatively, I may verbally request the cream and find that this response will also result in reinforcement— this time, however, because of the effects of my behavior ("please pass the cream") upon the behavior of others. Note that Skinner's definition does not limit verbal behavior to any limited group of responses, such as those involving the vocal tract. Nonvocal actions (gestures, facial expressions, etc.) often enable us to gain our ends through the behavior of others and hence qualify as verbal (but not vocal) behavior.

Skinner continually attempts to point out how a given class of verbal behavior might plausibly be explained in terms of some discriminative stimulus and reinforcement that jointly "control" the behavior (determine when it will occur). He attempts to classify verbal behavior into the various types of discriminative stimuli that "signal" the occasions when a given verbal response will be reinforced.

Perhaps the simplest class of verbal behavior Skinner calls the *mand*. Verbal statements such as *demands, commands,* or *requests* would all be classified as mands in his system. A specific mand might be our example above: "Please pass the cream." In this brief episode, Skinner would contend that the verbal response was partly controlled by the speaker's need for cream and partly by the presence of an audience. (The audience is regarded as an important discriminative stimulus; when there is no audience, when others are not within listening range, verbal behaviors are rarely if ever reinforced, and hence they rarely occur under these circumstances.) In attempting to account for the occurrence of the speaker's verbal response, Skinner would thus point to the probability that it had previously been successful in gaining reinforcements (cream) under similar circumstances and hence had gained in strength. Following this same approach, Skinner notes that if a polite request ("please") has typically increased the likelihood that mands will result in reinforcement, this term will probably accompany such statements in the future ("Please pass the cream"). If the word "please" has not generally enhanced the likelihood of reinforcement, it may well be omitted.

The *tact* represents a second major class of verbal behavior. In the case of the tact, the physical environment plays the role of discriminative stimulus. That is, the occurrence of the response depends upon certain characteristics of the environment. For example, Junior may call his mother, who is working in the yard, with the announcement that "there is a telephone call for you." The parent will generally reinforce this statement ("thank you") if, in fact, there has been a call; otherwise, the speaker's response will probably result in punishment rather than reinforcement. Thus, the physical environment partly determines Junior's verbal behavior; he learns to "match" his words with the state of affairs around him.

While a mand has obvious advantages for the speaker, the tact seems more for the benefit of the listener, since it may extend the listener's knowledge of his environment (without the speaker's announcement above, the listener would miss his call). Since tacts often provide him with valuable information, it is to the listener's advantage to reinforce them when they are properly executed. In this way, he may effectively strengthen the speaker's "informative" tacting behaviors and increase the frequency of their occurrence. However, there are many "true" tacts that the speaker will rarely emit, perhaps because they do *not* benefit his listening audience and hence have not been strengthened by previous reinforcements. For example, the speaker will usually refrain from "obvious" tacts that are uninformative to the listener ("The chair has four legs") since this behavior is not likely to have been reinforced in the past.

Two additional forms of verbal action are *textual* and *intraverbal*. Textual behavior denotes those instances in which a passage of written material serves as the discriminative stimulus that controls the speaker's utterances. In short, textual behavior refers to *reading*, a situation in which the speaker's responses are determined by the text to which he is exposed, presumably because of the reinforcements that may be gained through such behavior. To quote Skinner (p. 66), "If a child responds *cat* in the presence of the marks C-A-T and not otherwise, he receives approval."

Intraverbal behavior refers to instances in which the speaker's responses are determined by other verbal responses. For example, the question "How are you?" often elicits (is an occasion for) the response "Fine"; or the stimulus "Two times three" elicits "Six." Sometimes the speaker may supply his own stimulus for an intraverbal response, as when a singer, in attempting to recall a line somewhere in the middle of a song, finds it necessary to start from the beginning to get a "running start."

C. E. OSGOOD

While granting the importance of learning principles, many psychologists feel that Skinner's approach to verbal behavior is overly simple and cannot account for the extraordinary complexity of the phenomenon. Some have stressed the importance of meaning for an adequate understanding of language, for it is intuitively appealing to analyze language in terms of the correspondence between words and the things they represent—a correspondence technically referred to as *semantics*.

How do words come to acquire their meanings? Charles Osgood suggests (1957) that this occurs in two ways. At the most primitive level we have what he terms *sign learning*. In such cases, the child frequently hears a given word ("cat") in the presence of a specific object (the household cat). Through a process of conditioning, the *word* eventually comes to elicit some part of the child's response to the *object* (cat). While it is clear that we do not overtly respond in the same manner to the word and the object to which it refers, Osgood hypothesizes that the word does tend to elicit "light-weight" (that is, relatively easy-to-perform) components of the total response complex originally associated with the object, as shown diagrammatically in Figure 16. For example, while the object cat may elicit playful stroking behavior on the child's part, the word "cat" may result in an internal pattern of neural discharge (r_m) closely resembling the pattern (R_T) that occurs in response to the object cat. Moreover, the proprioceptive feedback (s_m) from these light-weight responses plays an important role in guiding the child's

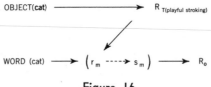

Figure 16

Osgood's theory of meaning. Following learning, the word "cat" elicits part of response complex originally associated with object cat. (Adapted from Osgood, C. E. Method and Theory in Experimental Psychology. *New York: Oxford University Press, 1953.)*

overt reaction (R_o) to any given word, as discussed earlier in connection with the phenomenon of mediated generalization (see p. 36).

In addition to *sign learning*, Osgood postulates that words often acquire their meaning by association with other signs whose meaning is already known; this is known as *assign learning*. He notes, for example, that most five-year-olds understand the word "ZEBRA," although they may never have been in the presence of a zebra. They have, however, been told of the zebra's various characteristics (size, shape, striped appearance, etc.); the reactions that the child has learned earlier to associate with these different characteristics are now "assigned" (through learning) to the new word "ZEBRA." Osgood assumes that a similar process is involved in learning the meaning of both signs and assigns; "light-weight" responses previously elicited by an *object* (in sign learning) or by a familiar *symbol* (in assign learning) now come to be associated with a new stimulus (word) through conditioning.

According to Osgood's theory, the learned mediating responses (r_m) associated with various words constitute their meaning. As shown in Figure 16, proprioceptive feedback (s_m) from these responses guides our overt reactions (R_o) to these language symbols. Unfortunately, however, the theory is quite vague in specifying the content and locus of these mediating responses—many of which may occur at a physiological or neurological level. Consequently, it has thus far been impossible to investigate the meaning process through direct observation. But there have been several attempts to deal quantitatively with meaning. Perhaps the best-known attempt is the semantic differential.

THE SEMANTIC DIFFERENTIAL

The semantic differential was developed as a method for measuring *connotative meaning* (associations called up when we are presented with various symbols), as contrasted with *denotative meaning* (objects and actions that these symbols represent in the real world). Thus while the words "nurse" and "teacher" may have similar *connotations* (helpful, kind, etc.) and hence would receive similar semantic differential profiles (see below), they *denote* persons in quite distinct occupational roles.

The semantic differential might best be described as a controlled association method for measuring connotative meaning. To determine the connotative meaning of a word like "justice," subjects might be asked to rate this word on a series of seven-step adjectival scales as shown in Figure 17. The responses (X's) in this example represent the

JUSTICE

CRUEL	:	:	:	:X:	:	_	KIND
CURVED	:	:	:	:X:	:		STRAIGHT
MASCULINE	:	:X:	:	:	:		FEMININE
ACTIVE	:	:	:	:X:	:		PASSIVE
SAVORY	:X:	:	:	:	:		TASTELESS
UNSUCCESSFUL	:	:X:	:	:	:		SUCCESSFUL

Figure 17

Responses to concept "justice" on several scales of semantic differential.

average ratings of 540 students at the University of Minnesota. It is assumed that the respondents' ratings indicate the extent to which they associate the different words being rated ("justice" in this case) with the various polar adjectives. In order to quantify such data it is common to assign the numbers 1 through 7 to the responses, depending upon the rating categories in which they fall; thus, if the value 1 was given to the "kind" end of the first scale, the concept "justice" would have a rating 3, while a neutral rating would be assigned a score of 4. Note again that this method does not enable us to determine the denotative meaning of justice, nor does it give us a good idea of what the dictionary definition might be. It does, however, indicate the attributes that our respondents associate with the concept of justice, and how strongly they hold to these associations. For example, within the Minnesota sample, justice is regarded as moderately kind (rather than cruel), moderately straight (as opposed to curved), moderately masculine, and so on.

An almost infinite variety of scales could be constructed by simply listing all the adjective-opposite pairs in a given language (for example, bright-dark, democratic-undemocratic, happy-sad, etc.). But Osgood, Suci, and Tannenbaum (1957) have found that different scales often elicit similar responses. For example, concepts rated as healthy (as opposed to sick) also tend to be rated as nice (rather than awful) and beautiful (rather than ugly). This cluster of scales and others like them are generally regarded as representing an *evaluative* factor, which essentially indicates how *good* versus *bad* a given concept seems to be. Thus, "justice" would be rated as healthy, nice, and beautiful, while "disgust" would be rated as sick, awful, and ugly. In addition to the evaluative cluster of scales, which seem to be the most numerous of all, Osgood and his collaborators have discovered two other important clusters representing *potency* and *activity*. The potency factor includes such scales as large-small, strong-weak, and heavy-light, while the activity cluster includes sharp-dull, hot-cold, and active-passive. Although recent research indicates that the realm of connotative meaning may include additional scale clusters (or dimensions) beyond the three listed, these three—evaluation, potency, and activity—represent important aspects of connotation in a wide variety of languages.

The semantic differential has proven to be a very flexible research tool; several of its applications are described below.

The Study of Compound Stimuli. One interesting application of the semantic differential is its use in the study of compound social stimuli. For example, Osgood and his collaborators (1957) have attempted to determine how the meanings of isolated adjectives and nouns such as "shy" and "scientist" are combined when they appear in the phrase "shy scientist." Thus, knowing that the adjective ("shy") is associated with a rather neutral evaluative meaning, while the noun ("scientist") has a more positive connotation, these investigators sought to determine how the individual evaluative meanings were combined to determine the meaning of the phrase "shy scientist."

Perhaps the most important and general finding in this study was the fact that in responding to the various pairs, the subjects tended to emphasize the adjectives more than the nouns. That is, while the typical adjective-noun pair might receive an evaluative rating somewhere between the ratings of its constituent elements, the adjective generally had a greater weight in determining the overall meaning of the pair. For example, if "shy" had received a neutral (4) rating on an evaluative scale such as good-bad, and "scientist" had received an extremely favorable rating of 1, the pair together ("shy scientist") might receive a mean rating of 3.0, instead of the 2.5 rating that would result from a simple average.

In another study concerning the judgment of compound stimuli, Manis, Gleason, and Dawes (1965) found evidence for an "extremity effect." Subjects in this experiment read several pairs of opinion statements concerning college fraternities. Both statements in each pair had presumably been endorsed by a single individual. Using a semantic differential scale that ranged from favorable to unfavorable, the subjects indicated the unknown person's attitude toward fraternities. For example, the subjects estimated the attitude of a student who had supposedly endorsed the statements:

College fraternities are hopelessly out of date.

and

The good and bad points of college fraternities balance each other.

The overall ratings were most clearly influenced by the more *extreme* component of each pair (the first statement in the above example), in contrast with the relatively weaker influence of the less extreme component. Although the evidence is not yet complete, it is possible that extreme attitude statements are given particular emphasis because the average person is confident that he knows how to interpret them correctly; that is, he feels relatively certain that he knows their appropriate position on a favorable-unfavorable continuum, while he feels uncertain in evaluating less polarized items.

Another type of compound stimulus investigated with the semantic differential is the combination of adverbs and adjectives. Consider an adjective like "disgusting" and the manner in which it is successively modified when preceded by such adverbs as "slightly," "somewhat," "very," or "extremely." Several investigators (Cliff, 1959; Howe, 1963) have concluded that in such adverb-adjective pairs the adverbs function as multipliers. That is, while an adverb like "slightly" is not associated with any particular quality (such as good or bad or active), it modifies the intensity of the adjectives with which it appears; thus, the strongly unfavorable connotations of a word like "disgusting" are reduced by about half in the phrase "slightly disgusting." Similarly, the favorable connotations of "charming" are reduced by half in the phrase "slightly charming." In general, we may predict that the favorability (or unfavorability) of the words "slightly *x*" (whatever adjective *x* may be—cruel or gifted or evil, etc.) will be about .5 times the favorability (or unfavorability) associated with *x* when it appears unmodified. Of course, other adverbs *intensify* adjectives that follow them. The word "extremely," for example, generally increases the favorability (or unfavorability) of its associated adjective by about 50 percent, and may therefore be assigned a value of 1.5. Thus, the phrase "extremely *x*" (whatever adjective *x* may be) will generally be rated as 1.5 times as favorable (or unfavorable) as the unmodified adjective *x*.

Psychotherapy. O. H. Mowrer used the semantic differential to quantify the changes in connotative meaning that accompanied psychotherapy (cited in Osgood et al., 1957). Two patients were represented in this exploratory study—a young man and a young woman. They were administered semantic differential forms on three occasions: near the start of therapy, at about the middle of the therapy process, and shortly after successful therapy had been terminated. The same eight concepts ("me," "mother," "father," "baby," "lady," "God," "sin," and "fraud") were rated in each of the three test sessions. By observing the similarity in the ratings given to the concepts "me," "father," and "mother," it was possible to assess the patients' identifications (did the young lady rate herself as being more similar to her father than her mother?). In Mowrer's cases, the young man initially saw himself as closely resembling his mother; and the young woman saw herself as resembling her father. By the end of therapy, however, the young man identified with his father, and the young woman with her mother. While the results of these two cases hardly constitute conclusive evidence about the effects of psychotherapy on parental identification, the method is promising, for the results seem sensible when compared with the therapist's clinical observations.

Semantic Satiation. Continued repetition or inspection of a word is often accompanied by a loss in the word's meaningfulness. You can informally investigate this phenomenon yourself, by looking at and concentrating on any of the words on this page (the word "page," for example).

To investigate this *semantic satiation* more systematically, some experimenters (Lambert and Jacobovits, 1960) have turned to the semantic differential. They reasoned that if continued inspection or repetition of a word leads to a loss in meaningfulness, this should be detectable in the semantic differential ratings elicited by the word. In particular, if a word loses its meaningfulness, it should be rated in more neutral terms than it was before the satiation procedure, since it would presumably become relatively devoid of connotative associations. Results of this sort have, in fact, been obtained in a series of studies.

Some related effects have also been observed. For example, if subjects continuously repeat a given word and are then asked to rate a synonym of this word, satiation effects may also be obtained for the synonym, suggesting that the satiation phenomenon has rather general cognitive ramifications, rather than being limited to single, isolated words. Also, where satiation procedures were applied to *numbers* which were then included as elements in various addition problems, the time required to solve these problems was effectively lengthened. In this case, presumably, satiation had temporarily reduced the meaningfulness of the numbers, and thus interfered with the subjects' ability to respond to the numbers appropriately in the test problems.

How are these results to be explained? Several conflicting explanations have been offered, perhaps the most popular being an inhibitory interpretation. This account emphasizes that most responses (verbal or otherwise) become temporarily less available immediately after being performed. If a rat has just turned left at the choice point of a T-maze, and is immediately placed in the maze again, the probability of his turning left again will be somewhat reduced. Moreover, if he has just been forced to take *several* left turns, the likelihood that he will turn left again will be still lower. Analogously, if we assume (as discussed earlier) that words and other symbols automatically result in certain internal mediating responses that constitute their meaning, we are led to anticipate that these meaning responses will be somewhat weaker and less available if they have just been repeatedly elicited. Thus, repetition of a word may make its associated meaning response less and less available, and would be reflected (a) in a relatively neutral semantic profile, and (b) in increased difficulty in solving problems requiring the use of these words.

GENERAL SEMANTICS

The general semantics movement was mainly stimulated by the writings of Alfred Korzybski, who inspired loyal disciples and attracted scornful academic critics. Korzybski (1933) felt that, through a rational analysis of language structures, it would be possible to discover some of the important roots of human behavior (both normal and abnormal), and to point the way to improving our individual lives and cultural heritage. He felt, for example, that the language behavior of psychotics, demagogues, and other confused individuals often violated semantic principles and revealed an all-too-common confusion of *words* with the *things* to which they refer. These difficulties could (hopefully) be corrected through application of the principles of general semantics.

One of Korzybski's most important points was thus the distinction between two types of meaning: *extensional* (or denotative) meaning and *intensional* (or connotative) meaning. The *extensional* meaning of a word is the "real-world" thing to which it refers. For example, in order to provide someone with the extensional meaning for the word "chicken" it would be necessary to show him, perhaps by pointing, just what this word refers to. The *intensional* meaning of a word, by contrast, is the set of associations that the word elicits. These associations may constitute a verbal equivalent of the word ("chicken is a domesticated fowl that is a popular food in the United States"). Intensional meanings may also be figurative, rather than literal; for example, the word "chicken" often implies cowardliness.

While every meaningful word has an intensional meaning, only certain words have extensional meaning. That is, certain words quite rich in their ability to elicit subjective associations may, nevertheless, be devoid of any "real-world" referents. When such nonextensional words are combined, the resulting statements may truly be considered "non-sense," for the truth or falsity of these assertions cannot be checked by sensory observation. Here is an example: "Angels are more honest than leprechauns." Note that it is impossible to cite empirical evidence that will have bearing on the truth or falsity of this statement, for two of the terms ("angel" and "leprechaun") do not exist in the same sense that tables, cows, and automobiles do, and hence are not available to be observed.

Since scientists in all fields are concerned with establishing facts and relationships that exist in the external, observable world, scientific language normally excludes nonextensional terms. In this way scientists avoid becoming involved in fruitless controversies that cannot be resolved by empirical (observational) means. In a similar vein, general semanticists suggested that social conflicts could often be avoided if we were all more "extensionally oriented," and hence focused on the events and relationships that exist in the external world, instead of on the subjective categories, labels, and stereotypes that constitute the world of intensional meaning. For example, in a discussion of the social position of Negroes in the United States, the extensional attitude would require a dispassionate emphasis upon the existing facts of life within the Negro community, rather than a subjective discourse (pro or con) based largely upon the discussants' associations and emotional reactions to the label "Negro." The extensional orientation would presumably result in some agreement on existing relevant facts, while an intensional approach would mainly result in a heated verbal exchange concerning the speakers' personal views, without reference to the "real world."

Granting for the moment the virtues of extensional language, a common problem occurs when a speaker uses a word that has one extensional meaning (referent) for him and another for his listener. A good illustration of this is that the term "political freedom" is used in a different sense in the United States than in the Soviet Union; that is, the two societies denote two quite distinct political systems by these words. Thus, while the Soviets may assert that communism guarantees political freedom, this assertion is clearly false if the phrase "political freedom" is interpreted as we understand it in the United States.

This example suggests that it is important for us to have extensional agreement concerning word meanings in order to avoid "semantic" disputes. In an effort to refine further the concept of extensional agreement, Johnson (1944) developed a quantitative measure of the degree to which different speakers associate a given word with the same referent. Here is how an extensional agreement index might be constructed for the words "statesman" and "vowel." Suppose 100 college students were presented with a list of United States senators and were asked to indicate those who qualified as "statesmen." Undoubtedly, we would find considerable disagreement among our respondents, indicating that they had different referents in mind when they used this word. We may contrast this anticipated outcome with the agreement that would undoubtedly emerge if our respondents were instructed to indicate senators whose last names began with a vowel. This agreement would be interpreted as evidence that our various respondents associated the term "vowel" with the same set of referents. We might thus conclude that if, in everyday speech, we were to use a term like "statesman," there would be a fairly good chance that our intended meaning would be misunderstood, since the listener's referent for this term might very well differ from the referent that we as speakers had intended. There would, however, be less likelihood of confusion when we used a word like "vowel." The implication here is obvious: if we wish to communicate most effectively, we should, whenever possible, use words whose extensional referent is widely agreed upon within our language community.

It is also possible to quantify *intensional agreement*. We would note the degree of agreement between various definitions (verbal equivalents) offered for a given word. We might, for example, compare the definitions that appear in different psychology texts for a word like "learning." After locating these definitions we would first eliminate all words except nouns, adjectives, verbs, and adverbs; we would then determine how many of the remaining words appeared in each of the definitions. If the same words were used in each of the definitions, we would conclude that intensional agreement was high; that is, we would have shown that there was a good deal of similarity between the word equivalents that the various texts offered for the term "learning." In one demonstration of this method it was found that biochemical terms tended to be defined in a more uniform manner from one book to the next than psychological terms were.

SYNTACTICS

Despite the heavy emphasis that psychologists have placed upon the concept of meaning (the study of semantics), language cannot be properly understood without an adequate conception of the ways in which words are ordered into sentences. Of course, numerous grammatical rules specify proper ways of constructing sentences in any language. However, these syntactic rules (the rules of word order) do not merely guard against awkward and ungrammatical speech, but also play a vital role in conveying the speaker's intended meaning. Consider the words "The boy hit the ball." These identical words can be rearranged to produce several quite distinct sentences—for example, "Hit the boy the ball"; "The ball hit the boy." Examples of this sort have led to the statement that the total linguistic meaning of a sentence is equal to the *lexical* (dictionary) meaning of its constituent words plus the *structural* meaning conveyed through the word order (Miller, 1954).

The importance of syntactic rules becomes still clearer when we recognize the "productive" characteristic of language. Adult mastery of a language normally enables the individual to speak and understand "original" sentences (sentences he has never heard or used before). This productive characteristic suggests that language behavior cannot be successfully explained by rote learning of sentences. George A. Miller (1964) has pointed to the possibility that with increased scientific understanding of the individual's implicit (not necessarily conscious) knowledge of the rules governing word order, we may be in a better position to explain the productive character of man's speech.

REDUNDANCY IN LANGUAGE

Since syntactic rules require that the speaker's utterances must conform to certain conventions of word order, and since these utterances will generally bear some sensible relationship to the "real world," it is often possible for the listener to *guess* some of the words that the speaker has used, even if he fails to hear exactly what has been said. By knowing the rules that guide the speaker's verbal behavior, the listener can thus infer what he has missed. For example, here is a passage from a contemporary novel in which every fifth word has been deleted. See if you can guess the words deleted.

The glory of Manhattan ___(1)___ Willie had seen from ___(2)___ airplane was nowhere visible ___(3)___ Broadway and Fiftieth Street ___(4)___ he came up out ___(5)___ the subway. It was ___(6)___ same old dirty crowded ___(7)___ : here a cigar store, ___(8)___ an orange-drink stand, ___(9)___ a flickering movie marquee. . . .[1]

As you can see, in this ordinary passage of English text, many of the constituent words are readily predictable from the context in which they appear. Words that can be successfully guessed from their context are termed redundant, since the presence of these words does not convey much beyond what is implied by the surrounding verbal context. Languages generally contain a great deal of redundancy. This often enables the speaker to convey his meaning even though some parts of his message may have been lost in transmission due to noise, faulty pronunciation, or his listener's inattention.

Two types of experiments provide clear evidence that redundancy tends to eliminate errors in communication. One study (Miller, Heise, and Lichter, 1951) was concerned with the effect of redundancy on the intelligibility of speech. The subjects were presented with a series of words tape-recorded against a noisy background. The subjects simply had to indicate the words they heard. The results showed that words presented in a meaningful sentence were easier to understand and correctly identify than they were when presented in random order. When a word is placed within a sentence, such as, "Apples grow on ————," there is a limited range of possibilities for the missing word. Even a vague impression

---

[1] The correct answers are: (1) which, (2) the, (3) on, (4) when, (5) of, (6) the, (7) street, (8) there, and (9) yonder. From *The Caine Mutiny* by Herman Wouk. Copyright 1951 by Herman Wouk. Reprinted by permission of Doubleday & Company, Inc.

of the last word enables the listener to make a fairly good guess. On the other hand, when words are presented in isolation there is no redundancy, and the listener finds it difficult to guess correctly when he is uncertain of a word, for the range of possibilities is virtually limitless.

A study by Taylor (1953) suggests that redundancy also affects the receiver's ability to *comprehend* a message; that is, highly redundant messages are more apt to convey successfully their meaning than are messages low in redundancy. Taylor's study was conducted as follows: In order to measure the redundancy of several written passages, he employed a procedure known as the "Cloze" technique (derived from the Gestalt concept of closure; see Weintraub and Walker on *Perception*). As shown in our passage above from *The Caine Mutiny*, Taylor simply deleted every fifth word of the original material and had a group of students attempt to fill in the missing words. For passages that were readily understandable, it was relatively easy to replace the deleted words; for other passages—particularly those difficult to comprehend— the missing words were hard to guess. Taylor's results thus indicated that the readability of a written passage was related to its redundancy. Passages that were most readable (easiest to understand) were more redundant than those that proved to be relatively difficult.

ON COMPREHENSIBLE WRITING

Taylor's findings concerning the relationship between verbal redundancy and readability warrant further amplification, since many people are concerned with making their writing more comprehensible. At a practical level, we might inquire into some of the characteristics that typically appear in prose that is easy to understand. In brief, how can the writer tell when his prose is reasonably redundant (and hence comprehensible) without subjecting it to the complexities of the Cloze procedure?

Two main factors seem to play an important role here. One of these is the writer's use of familiar words. Not surprisingly, familiar words are relatively easy to understand; and generally speaking, the more familiar the words, the more comprehensible the passage. Familiar words also make for redundancy. Consider a passage that contains many difficult words like "amanuensis" or "ubiquitous." When uncommon words of this sort are deleted in the course of the Cloze procedure, most readers will find it difficult to guess what has been omitted. Consequently, passages that contain many difficult words turn out to be low in redundancy; and as we have seen, low redundancy usually leads to poor comprehension.

A second factor that affects both redundancy and reading comprehension is the average sentence length within the passage. Long sentences tend to produce passages low in redundancy and difficult to comprehend.

Long sentences often arrange words in patterns that are strange to the reader's verbal habits, whereas short sentences cannot. In a long sentence the qualifications can split apart words that function together. The reader's memory span is limited, and he is apt to forget the noun before he discovers the verb that goes with it (Miller, *Language and Communication*, p. 37).

Several methods have now been devised to provide the writer with systematic help in determining the readability of his prose. These techniques typically require a careful analysis of word familiarity and sentence length, among other factors. The so-called Flesch count is perhaps the most widely used of these procedures.[2]

THE STATISTICAL APPROACH TO LANGUAGE

Despite our everyday familiarity with speech and writing, there are certain statistical regularities in language that we rarely note, but which have been the object of intensive study by various researchers. These regularities are often uncovered by simple counting procedures; for example, written or spoken communication may be analyzed by counting the frequency with which different words appear. One of the more important findings uncovered through this technique is Zipf's *Law of Least Effort* (1949). According to this law, the more effort involved in emitting a given word (or sound), the less frequent the appearance of that word in everyday discourse. One index of "word effort" would, of course, be the length of the word; in general, we may assume that long words require more effort than short ones. The law of least effort thus suggests that, on the average, short words will be used more often than long ones. This relationship between word length and word frequency has in fact been verified in Chinese, Latin, and English, suggesting that it is probably characteristic of all languages.

In interpreting these data, Zipf argues that frequent usage causes the shortening of words. Examples such as the shortening of "moving pictures" to "movies," and "automobile" to "auto" or "car" illustrate this trend. Another example is the widespread use of abbreviations for the various government agencies—a trend that is particularly prominent

---

[2] The Flesch count is computed by randomly selecting several sample passages—each containing 100 words—from the material being scored. The average number of syllables within each 100-word passage is then determined; this provides an indirect measure of *word familiarity* (W), since—as noted in Zipf's research described in the next section—unfamiliar words tend to be long and have many syllables. The average number of *words per sentence* (S) within these 100-word samples is also computed. Reading ease is then quantified by the formula:

$$\text{Reading ease} = 206.84 - 0.85W - 1.02S$$

Passages that score below 60 on this measure are fairly difficult to read, and scores around zero indicate impossibly difficult material. Scores of 80 and above generally indicate easy reading.

among federal employees in Washington, D.C. As you might guess, the everyday activities of government workers require them to talk about these agencies on many occasions. Hence, according to Zipf's law, they should show a strong inclination to shorten the formal names of the agencies. The Department of Health, Education and Welfare is thus colloquially referred to as HEW, while the Organization of American States is abbreviated to the OAS. The development of slang and specialized scientific jargon often seems to follow a similar pattern. Note, for example, the use of the term GSR, rather than galvanic skin response, among research psychologists.

Sapir (1916) argued that the length of a word also gives us a clue about the age of the word. In particular, Sapir suggested that short words are generally *old* ones, while new words are more likely to be long "compounds" formed by the combination of several short "kernels." For example, such short words as "knight," "good," and "sun" have doubtless been a part of the English language for a considerable time, as contrasted with words of more recent origin like "television" or "delicatessen." If Zipf is correct, we may expect that these new, rather long words will eventually become shorter—at least among those who have occasion to use them frequently. Perhaps we are already seeing the start of this process in the emergence of the colloquial terms "telly" and "delly."

INTERPRETING PERSUASIVE MESSAGES

Everyday speech abounds with statements of opinion. People are continually conversing about their views on a variety of topics, ranging from foreign policy to the current state of popular music. Some of these statements are intended to convince others of the validity of our views. In this way, the speaker may gain consensual validation for his beliefs; he may become more confident that his views are warranted if he can successfully convince others of their merit. Other statements of opinion may simply result from inquiries: "What did you think of today's lecture?"

Regardless of its source, a statement of opinion is an attempt to inform the listener of the speaker's point of view. A simplified way to look at this is to conceive of the speaker as occupying some position along a scale that runs from extreme favorability to extreme unfavorability. If, for example, he is moderately unfavorable toward Dixieland jazz, we may think of him as being somewhere on the negative side of the scale, although not at the extreme. When this speaker tries to explain his position ("I find it difficult to get excited about Dixieland. . . . It seems sort of out of date"), he is essentially providing the listener with information concerning his preferred location on this evaluative continuum. The listener, on the other hand, must interpret the speaker's statement and arrive at a conclusion concerning just how favorable or unfavorable an attitude it reflects. Take the above statement about Dixieland, for example; if a rating of "1" represented an extremely *favorable* attitude and "7" represented an extremely *unfavorable* attitude, what numerical rating should we assign to a person who had made this comment? Should we give him a 5 or a 6 or what?

If our language were completely unambiguous, such statements should enable us unhesitatingly to infer just how unfavorable are the speaker's underlying views. Moreover, in an ideal language, a given statement of opinion would be given the same interpretation by all listeners. As we shall see, although our language usually enables the listener to make a gross judgment of the speaker's views (pro or anti), the listener's own attitudes often affect his interpretation of what appears to be a simple and direct statement of opinion.

Let us therefore consider the influence of the listener's views on the interpretations that he places upon statements of opinion. Several studies have now been completed on this question; one of the most famous (Hovland, Harvey, and Sherif, 1957) was conducted in Oklahoma during a campaign to repeal the prohibition laws in that state. The investigators first selected several groups of people who held quite divergent views concerning the dangers of alcohol. Some of these people were members of the WCTU; others were active in the campaign to loosen the prohibition regulations; and still others were essentially neutral. People from these various groups were all presented with a persuasive message that took a mildly anti-prohibition stand, and were asked to indicate the writer's preferred position along a pro-prohibition to anti-prohibition scale. The results indicated that there were systematic differences between the various groups with respect to their understanding of the writer's views. People whose own beliefs were relatively similar to the views presented in the message generally minimized what little difference there was; that is, they interpreted the message as being even closer to their own beliefs than was actually the case. This type of distortion, in which the meaning of a message is "displaced" toward the receiver's preferred position, has been termed the *assimilation effect*. Not all subjects showed assimilation, however. Those whose views clearly conflicted with the contents of a message typically exaggerated the existing discrepancy by interpreting the message as being even more opposed to their views than in fact it was. This type of distortion, in which the speaker's intended meaning is displaced *away* from the recipient, has been termed the *contrast effect*.

How might we explain these results? What are the underlying mechanisms? Unfortunately, there is no clear agreement. One theory (Manis, 1961) suggests that these distortions mainly result from the recipients' attempts to reduce the impact of the message on their *own* beliefs. The underlying notion here holds that the receiver of a message usually feels some pressure to change his views when he hears them attacked. Moreover, as the message diverges more and more from his own beliefs, he feels increasing pressure to change. Eventually, when the discrepancy between his own views and those embodied in the message becomes sufficiently large, the listener may feel less pressure to change. This is most likely to happen when the message source is unknown to the recipient, for under these conditions, if a statement of opinion is clearly at variance with the recipient's views, the unidentified speaker will be readily dismissed as a "crackpot" or some otherwise misguided individual whose divergent beliefs may be comfortably ignored.

What does all this have to do with message distortion? Figure 18 shows how these assumptions enable us to explain assimilation and con-

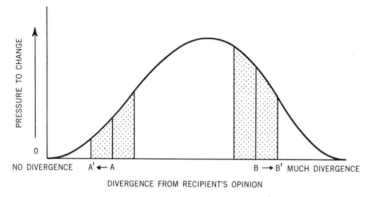

Figure 18

Pressure to change as affected by divergence of opinion between speaker and recipient. This diagram assumes that speaker's identity is unknown to recipient. Displacement effects from A to A' (assimilation) and from B to B' (contrast) result from attempt to minimize pressure to change.

trast effects. In this graph, the horizontal axis represents various degrees of discrepancy between the views of the receiver and those of the speaker. The vertical axis shows the amount of pressure to change that the recipient would normally feel upon receiving persuasive messages that differ from his own views by these varying amounts. Assume, for example, that the recipient favors an extremely pro-fraternity position at the extreme left of the horizontal axis. As you can see, we have assumed that pressure to change first rises and then falls, as he receives incoming messages that diverge more and more from his preferred pro-fraternity stand. Since an incoming message is almost always ambiguous (to a greater or lesser degree), the receiver must generally choose from a range of "possible" interpretations. Moreover, since he is generally motivated to maintain his existing views with little or no change, it is reasonable to predict that each message will be interpreted in such a manner as to minimize the resulting pressure to change. Consider a message that, given a *proper interpretation*, might be moderately discrepant with the listener's views; the "true meaning" of this message might be at position A in Figure 18. While a range of *possible* interpretations might be given to this message, as shown by the gray area of the graph, the model suggests that our hypothetical recipient will probably interpret the message as espousing position A′, rather than position A, since messages at A′ are associated with less pressure to change. Note also that the displacement from A to A′ constitutes an *assimilation effect*, since it reduces the apparent discrepancy between the receiver's views and those that he attributes to the message source.

Figure 18 also shows how contrast might occur. Consider a message that deviates markedly from the receiver's views; assume that its actual location is B. As before, we assume that there is some ambiguity concerning the communicator's true position, as indicated by the gray area. Since, according to our model, the recipient should choose the interpretation that minimizes pressure to change, we are led to predict that the message will be interpreted as advocating position B′, rather than position B, thus resulting in a *contrast effect*. Note that, as in our example of assimilation, this distorted interpretation helps the recipient to maintain his own views, for it effectively reduces the pressure to change that the message will generate.

While assimilation and contrast have frequently been reported in studies of this sort, they do not always appear, nor should they, according to the theory proposed above. First, let us recall that in our previous examples we have always assumed that the author of the message is unknown to the receiver, and that as a consequence, messages seen as being highly discrepant with his views may be largely discounted since they may be interpreted as "proof" that the source is not trustworthy. Obviously, however, in many instances the author's identity is well known. How might this affect our results? Consider, for example, a speaker who is well liked and respected by his audience. Under these conditions, regardless of the discrepancy between the message content and the views of the listener, it is unlikely that the speaker's opinion will be discounted. Indeed, there is considerable evidence to show that under these "high-prestige" conditions, the recipient of a persuasive message feels more and more pressure to change his views, as the incoming message shows increasing divergence from his preferred stand.

Figure 19 graphically depicts this state of affairs. As in our previous examples, let us now assume that our recipient is presented with messages at positions A and B, remembering that in this case he knows that the communicator is a person worthy of his respect. As before, the messages

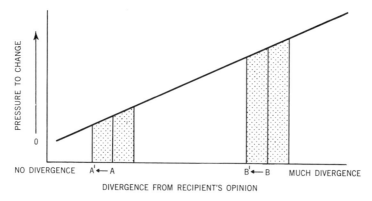

Figure 19

Pressure to change as affected by divergence of opinion between speaker and recipient. This diagram assumes that speaker is trusted and respected by recipient. Displacement effects from A to A' and from B to B' (both instances of assimilation) result from attempt to minimize pressure to change.

are assumed to be somewhat ambiguous, thus permitting a variety of interpretations. Note that under these conditions, for both messages A and B, pressure to change can be most effectively minimized by a displacement *toward* the recipient's preferred stand (to A' and B')—in short, assimilation. It should also be noted that, according to this interpretation, contrast effects should *never* be obtained when the speaker is highly regarded by his audience. Regardless of how discrepant his message may be when compared with the recipients' views, assimilation effects should always be obtained, since this type of displacement will consistently reduce the listener's tendency to change his views.

A study by Manis (1961a) reports results in good agreement with these predictions. In this experiment, several groups of college students who varied in their attitudes toward college fraternities were presented with a series of short essays, each of which described the author's views on the fraternity issue. Although the authors were not personally known to the subjects, they were described in rather glowing terms. Some were said to be excellent students, others were described as very popular, and still others were described as being exceptionally stable and personally mature. When the subjects attempted to infer the authors' attitudes toward fraternities after having read their messages, clear-cut assimilation effects were obtained regardless of the discrepancy between the readers' views and those of the authors. That is, there was a consistent tendency for the pro-fraternity subjects to interpret the messages as being more pro-fraternity than did those who opposed fraternities. It is interesting to note that when these same messages were presented as coming from less reliable sources, no consistent relationship was found between the subjects' own views and their interpretations of the messages. One might have expected that this would lead to consistent *contrast effects*, in that many people prefer to believe that their own views are rather different from the views of those they hold in low esteem. However, a subsequent study (Berkowitz and Goranson, 1964), contrast effects were obtained when persuasive messages were attributed to a disliked source. Taken as a whole, these results testify to the importance of such "nonmessage" variables as the recipient's attitudes and the author's status as determinants of message interpretation. As suggested above, these factors should ideally be irrelevant in the communication process. As we have seen, however, human communication is often less than ideal.

INVOLVEMENT AND MESSAGE INTERPRETATION

People differ not only in their *attitudes* toward various social institutions, but they may also differ in the degree to which a given issue *involves* them. That is, while some people may be highly favorable to the cause of civil rights, this may not be a particularly important issue for them; others with equally favorable attitudes may be more involved in civil rights, and may thus take a more active role in advancing their views.

An experiment conducted at the University of North Carolina (Ward, 1965) sought to determine if differences in involvement had any impact upon the individual's interpretation of opinion statements. In this study, three groups of subjects were presented with a series of statements concerning the Negro in the United States, and were asked to rate each statement according to the favorability of its content. While the three groups were all pro-Negro, they differed in involvement. Some of the students had actively participated in the picketing of local movie theaters in an attempt to eliminate segregated seating. Prior to the experiment half of these "picketers" were reminded of their membership in this group. Hence it may be assumed that these people were maximally involved while participating in the study, both because of their voluntary picketing activity and because the experimenter had made their membership in this group a salient matter. The group next highest in involvement was comprised of people who had picketed the theaters, but were led to believe that their selection for the study had occurred through chance; that is, their picketing membership was not made salient during the course of the experiment. The third, and least-involved group, was composed of pro-Negro students who had *not* participated in the movie picketing and whose attitudes were not salient at the time of the experiment. The results indicated that involvement in the Negro issue resulted in a consistent contrast effect—a displacement of the statements away from the subject's own position. That is, among these subjects, all of whom were pro-Negro, those who were most involved in the topic at hand interpreted the statements of opinion as being less favorable to the Negro than did those who were relatively uninvolved. In a sense, these results suggest that the involved individual is very "choosy" before agreeing that a given statement actually belongs on the side of the continuum he favors. That is, he may have what has been referred to as an "elevated threshold" of acceptance, while the less involved individual may be less critical before concluding that a statement is in essential agreement with his views.

THE PERSPECTIVE EFFECT

In some situations, the receiver of a persuasive message is not especially concerned with any *single* speaker's views on a given issue, but is, instead, trying to compare the views of two speakers to see if they share the same attitudes. Consider the average voter who knows something about the public statements of several political figures and who is trying to determine the extent to which they agree, rather than trying to estimate how pro or con their individual views might be. Informal social observation in this type of setting suggests that most people are very quick to detect attitudinal differences among those with whom they are in general agreement. For example, people who are extremely conservative are generally quite sensitive to the differences between such progressive Republicans as former President Eisenhower and such conservative Republicans as the late Senator Robert Taft. For the extreme liberal, on the other hand, the differences between these two figures may be more difficult to detect. Analogously, the conservative often fails to notice the difference between the views of a Socialist like Norman Thomas and those advocated by a liberal Democrat, while the distinction here may be quite clear to someone of more liberal bent. What we are describing might be termed a "perspective effect," since it refers to the manner in which the judge's attitudinal position (or perspective) affects his ability to notice differences between the views of others.

We should hasten to add that the evidence for a perspective effect is not limited to the sort of casual observations noted above. Ager and Dawes (1965) have studied this phenomenon in a more systematic manner. These investigators first selected two groups of subjects—one favorably disposed toward science and one opposed to science. All subjects were presented with several pairs of statements proclaiming similar, but not identical, views about science. The subjects were to indicate which statement from each pair reflected the more favorable attitude. In the following—a pair of statements used by Ager and Dawes—which would you select as most pro-science?

(1) A scientific analysis should always be preferred to any other.
(2) Through science alone will man comprehend the universe.

Since the correct answers to the various statement-pairs had previously been determined by obtaining the judgments of a large *unselected* group (including people of diverse attitudes), it was a simple matter to score the subjects' responses. In the pair presented above, for example, statement number 2 was considered to be more pro-science by most respondents. Not all subjects agreed with this choice, however. In general, when both members of a statement-pair came from the pro-science end of the attitude scale (as in the above example), people who were *themselves* pro-science rarely made an error, while those who opposed science made many errors. For pairs of statements that were mainly antiscience, however, most of the errors were made by subjects who favored science. The results of this study thus clearly demonstrate the existence of a "perspective effect" and suggest that people can most readily detect minimal differences between statements with which they agree. As a result, they find it simple to evaluate correctly the differences between statements they favor, while they show poor judgment in assessing the differences between statements with which they disagree.

SUMMARY

1. Language behavior has fascinated scholars from diverse disciplines, and they have studied it from a variety of vantage points. B. F. Skinner has attempted to explain man's verbal behavior by stressing the importance of such concepts as reinforcement and the discriminative stimulus, which have previously been shown to be important determinants of nonverbal behavior. For Skinner, the main difference between verbal and nonverbal behavior is that verbal responses are typically reinforced because of their effects upon another person, while nonverbal behavior operates directly upon the environment.

2. Charles Osgood has stressed the way in which verbal meanings are developed through the association between words and things. His theory assumes that, through conditioning, a word eventually comes to elicit a part of the total behavior pattern initially associated with the thing it signifies.

3. To investigate the process of connotative meaning, Osgood developed an instrument known as the semantic differential, which is essentially a controlled association technique that may be used to quantify the individual's symbolic reactions to verbal (or nonverbal) stimuli. The semantic differential measures three aspects of connotative meaning: evaluation, potency, and activity. It has proven to be a useful tool in a great range of investigations.

4. The general semanticists have emphasized the distinction between words and the things they signify. They have also identified two types of meaning: *extensional* meaning (the "real-world" thing to which a word

refers) and *intensional* meaning (the individual's subjective associations to the word). The general semanticists feel that we have often generated needless individual and social confusion by confusing words and things and failing to adopt an extensional attitude while communicating.

5. While semantics is concerned with the relationship between words and things, syntactics deals with the rules governing word order. These rules not only enable us to speak in a "correct" and grammatical manner, but they also play a vital role in conveying the speaker's intended meaning, for by simply rearranging the words in a given sentence we may change its meaning quite drastically.

Since syntactic rules require verbal utterances to conform to certain conventions of word order, it is often possible to guess some of the words that a speaker will use from the verbal context in which they appear. Words whose occurrence can be successfully anticipated simply from their context are termed *redundant*. Redundancy facilitates communication since it often enables the listener to infer what the speaker is saying even if he fails to hear some of the words in the message. Redundancy also makes messages easier to understand.

6. Short words tend to occur more frequently than long ones. In his Law of Least Effort, Zipf contends that frequency of usage eventually affects the word length, rather than vice versa. In a related vein, Sapir has suggested that short words tend to be of ancient origin, while long ones are often compounds formed by the amalgamation of older "kernels."

7. Persuasive messages are often given diverse interpretations, depending upon the attitudes and involvement of the listener, and the apparent status of the message source. It is clear, then, that in interpreting a message, we are affected by more than just the simple constituent words. Two important findings noted in this connection are *assimilation* (the tendency to displace the communicator's intended meaning toward one's own preferred position) and *contrast* (the tendency to exaggerate the discrepancy between one's own views and those of the communicator).

Typically, thinking involves internal mechanisms not directly observable. A person seated almost motionless in a study hall may be actively thinking about a problem in statistics, and yet from our external vantage point we cannot examine his thought processes directly.

As a rule, the *discovery* of a correct mode of response is of prime importance in thinking. Puzzles, riddles, and scientific problems—and other tasks generally regarded as involving thought—typically place maximum demands upon the individual's ability to discover the "right answer." Learning situations, in contrast, often provide the correct answer in a rather direct form (as when the child learns the multiplication table). Thought processes often seem to develop quite suddenly. For example, after repeatedly failing to solve a mechanical puzzle, an individual may suddenly discover the correct solution; and having mastered the problem just once, he may have little difficulty when it is presented a second time. In contrast, the child who has correctly given the product of "2×2" for the first time (following a memorization period) may yet make subsequent errors before mastering the problem completely. These observations suggest that the successful thinker may rapidly move from a state in which he does not know the solution to a problem, to a second state in which he knows the solution well, with no intermediate transitions such as we often encounter in learning situations. This rapid spurt in performance is the main characteristic of *insight*—an almost instantaneous reorganization of the elements in a problem situation, leading to successful solution. Comic strips generally depict insight with the time-worn symbol of the electric light bulb suddenly lighting inside the thinker's head.

One last feature of thought that we should consider is its generality. Some investigators have suggested that generality may be a prime feature distinguishing *reproductive* thinking (simple learning of correct responses) from *productive* thinking. With productive thinking, when a person has succeeded in solving a given problem, he should be able immediately to generalize his solution to other problems of the same class. For example, suppose I present the following series of equations to an adolescent who has not yet learned about squaring: $2^2 = 4$, $3^2 = 9$, $4^2 = 16$. I then ask him to tell me what 5^2 equals. Through *reproductive thinking* (simple learning) he may succeed in remembering the numerical values equal to 2^2, 3^2, and 4^2 but be unable to give the value of 5^2. If, however, our adolescent has grasped the underlying principle of the problem through *productive thinking,* he will be able to generalize the information he has been given, so that he can provide us with the correct answer to a great variety of squaring problems—for example, 5^2, 9^2, 10^2, etc.

LEARNING AND THINKING

The distinction between thinking and learning has troubled psychologists for many years. Historically, one of the most famous experiments concerning this distinction was Thorndike's (1898) study of cats in a problem box. Thorndike placed each of his cats in a cagelike apparatus from which they could escape if they would first perform some predetermined response, such as pulling a string or turning a door latch. On observing the animals' resultant behavior, Thorndike was struck by the lack of any clearly identifiable evidence of planned thinking. In the main, they seemed to respond in a rather undirected fashion until, usually by "accident," they would hit upon the correct response and escape from their confinement. It is important to note that when placed in the box once again (following a successful escape), they did not show evidence of insight; they did not act as if they had "caught on" to the solution to their dilemma, but returned to their seemingly unintelligent thrashing about before repeating the correct response for the second time. With repeated trials, of course, the animals would perform appropriately almost immediately after being placed in the box, but this speed of response developed gradually.

For Thorndike, then, the behavior of his animals seemed to be characterized by an initial period of almost random behavior followed by the *accidental* performance of the correct response; after this accidental discovery, the law of effect (p. 10) led to a gradual strengthening of the appropriate solution until this response came to dominate consistently the other possible modes of action.

Note that Thorndike's account does not seem to require any assumption that the animal's escape results from thinking. For one thing, the original discovery of the correct response seemed to be an accident. Moreover, even after this first performance of the correct response, the cats seemed to require many repetitions before they would turn to the response without delay, suggesting that they were gradually *learning* how to behave, rather than discovering through insight that their accidental response was the route to escape.

THINKING AND INSIGHT

In contrast to Thorndike's trial-and-error account of thinking, Wolfgang Köhler (1925), a famous Gestalt psychologist, placed considerable emphasis on the importance of planning and insight. He argued that

Thorndike's experiment was inappropriate for studying problem solving, since from the animal's viewpoint it was virtually impossible to arrive at a solution through foresightful planning. For example, the animal could not understand the workings of the trick doors Thorndike often used, since certain important aspects of the release mechanism might be placed outside the animal's field of vision. Secondly, Köhler pointed out that Thorndike's problems typically required a response that was not natural for his animal subjects (turning a door latch, for example). The fact that these responses were somewhat foreign to the animal's normal repertoire meant that they could be discovered only by sheer chance.

In Köhler's own studies, which were conducted with apes and chimpanzees, all of the elements necessary for solution were placed in clear sight. One of his most famous experiments involved placing a chimp's food for the day out of his reach, suspended from the top of the cage. However, a box in the cage could be moved under the food and used as a platform, enabling the animal to obtain his meal easily. Several of Köhler's chimps seemed to show insight. Instead of responding in a random, unthinking manner until they accidentally "stumbled" onto the solution, they seemed suddenly to "discover" the correct response, which they then carried out with speed and directness. The main evidence for insight here was the fact that the solution seemed to follow from a foresightful plan. Moreover, when placed in the situation once again after the initial solution, the animal solved the problem immediately, and did not exhibit the slow trial-by-trial improvement that Thorndike had observed. In contrast to Thorndike's emphasis on learning, Köhler contended that successful problem solving was mostly a matter of insight and perceptual reorganization (seeing how the elements of the problem might be related), and could not readily be explained in terms of prior experience.

In one case, when an animal did not succeed in getting to the food after a full day of fruitless attempts, Köhler demonstrated the solution by placing the box in an appropriate position, standing on it, and then reaching up to the food. Although this animal had apparently been unable to discover the solution without aid, he immediately understood (perceived?) the significance of Köhler's demonstration, for he was subsequently able to solve the problem without requiring direct reinforcement for his *own* behavior.

How are we to reconcile the findings of Thorndike with those of Köhler? Is problem solving a trial-and-error affair, or does insight play an important role? One might, of course, be tempted to accept both these conflicting accounts as possible because Thorndike primarily studied cats, while Köhler worked with phylogenetically higher-level animals, chimpanzees. However, this proposed solution seems unsatisfactory, for several experiments have shown insightful behavior even in the lowly rat (Maier, 1929).

Some investigators have suggested that learning and insight may be more closely related than they seem at first glance. For example, Birch (1945) has demonstrated the importance of past experience in the development of insight. In Birch's experiment, chimpanzees were presented with a problem situation in which some food was placed beyond reach, outside their cage. They were, however, given a hoe with which they could reach the food and rake it into range. Of the six animals that Birch tested, four were unable to solve the problem (of the other two, one solved it "accidentally," using a trial-and-error method, while the other seemed to show insight). To demonstrate the role of experience, Birch next presented his animals with some short straight sticks that they played with for three days. During this time, they gradually learned through trial and error to use the sticks for prying, shoveling, and poling. When the chimpanzees were then re-tested with the hoe problem, they were able to solve it with relative ease. Studies like this suggest that insight may be built upon a network of simple habits learned in the past; without these earlier experiences, problems are more likely to be solved through trial-and-error methods, if they are solved at all.

A series of famous experiments by Harlow (1949) provided further evidence that insight depends upon previous trial-and-error learning. Perhaps the simplest experiment of this series involved a straightforward discrimination learning test. Monkeys were presented with a board on which were placed two objects that differed in size, shape, and color. On each presentation the monkey was to choose one of the objects; if its choice was correct it was rewarded, for under one object in each pair the experimenter had previously placed some raisins or peanuts. A given pair of objects would be presented over and over, in different positions on the board; the reward could always be found under the same object. When the monkey had finally learned which object of the pair he was to choose (that is, when he could choose the correct object on every trial), a *new* pair of objects was presented. With the new pair of objects, the monkey was given another series of trials in which he could earn a reward by choosing the correct object; as before, trials were continued until the problem was mastered. By presenting a long series of different discrimination problems, Harlow was able to observe dramatic changes in the animals' problem-solving behavior. In brief, while the early problems were learned through laborious trial and error, the animals gradually developed their learning capabilities until they eventually showed a type of insight; they could respond to a new problem with near-perfect accuracy after only one trial. (The first response to each problem was, of course, a "guess," since the animals had no way of knowing in advance which of the two objects in a pair had been designated as correct.) Figure 20 shows the results of this study in graphic form. Note that the per-

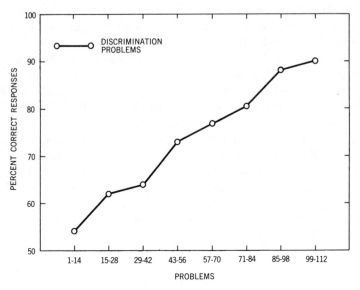

Figure 20

Development of learning set. Graph shows steady increase in percentage of correct responses on second trial of successive problems. (Adapted from Harlow, 1949.)

centage of correct responses on the second trial of each problem showed a steady rise as the animals gained additional experience in problem solving. Thus, on the second trial of the *early* problems, the animals responded correctly somewhere between 50 and 55 percent of the time; by problems 99–112, on the other hand, their performance on the second trial had risen to a level of about 90 percent correct.

In discussing his results, Harlow contended that the ability to solve problems in an insightful manner is *not* an innate capacity, but is instead gradually developed through learning. He thus suggested that by solving problems we gradually learn how to learn—that is, we develop "learning sets" and gradually acquire problem-solving skills that may be applied to future problems. For example, when faced with a pair of objects from which to choose, Harlow's monkeys may have learned to follow an implicit strategy of "win-stay, lose-switch" (if a previous choice has been correct, stay with it on the next trial; if it was incorrect, the choice should be switched for the next trial). Such an approach might reasonably evolve during learning, for it would constitute an adaptive strategy that could be profitably applied regardless of the particular pair of objects presented.

Harlow further suggested that in previous investigations of insightful behavior in animals and humans, the researchers knew very little of the early history of the experimental subjects. As a result, it was quite possible that the insight observed represented the result of a long learning period, during which problem-solving skills had been gradually acquired.

THOUGHT AND LANGUAGE

What are the building blocks of thought? This complex and difficult question cannot be answered with any certainty. However, many psychologists have suggested that there is an intimate connection between language and thought. John B. Watson, the founder of the behaviorist school of psychology, was one of the early advocates of this position. He objected to the use of such "subjective" terms as "thoughts," "ideas," and "images," for these concepts could not be readily employed in an approach that insisted upon *observable* stimuli and responses. (How can an experimenter see his subjects' ideas?) Watson's position led him to the view that thinking is a "materialistic" activity something like speaking, except the thinker restrains himself from overt expression. Thus, thinking was to be regarded as subvocal or implicit speech.

Max (1935, 1937) has collected what probably constitutes the best evidence in support of this theory. He investigated the thought processes of deaf-mutes. Unlike normal people, deaf-mutes "talk" with their fingers, and Watson's theory would therefore suggest that thinking should be closely associated with finger movements among a group of deaf subjects, but not within a group of normal people. To assess his subjects' finger movements—which according to Watson's theory might occur on a very minute level—Max constructed an electrical recording device that enabled him to detect very small electrical changes in the muscles that control the fingers. By means of this apparatus it was possible to observe muscular changes too minute to produce observable movements. In one study, subjects were trained to fall asleep while recordings were being taken. Max noted that sleep was generally accompanied by a decrease in the recordable activity. For the deaf subjects, muscular activity during sleep typically coincided with dream episodes. For the normal (nonmute) subjects, dreaming was *not* necessarily associated with bursts of activity. In another experiment, Max found that his deaf-mutes showed more activity in their fingers than did normals when they were asked to solve various problems "in their heads."

Max's observations thus tend to support Watson's view, for they essentially point to an association between mental effort and muscular activity in the "speech" apparatus. However, this evidence falls short of "proving" that implicit speech is the basis for all thinking. It might be contended, for example, that the muscular changes observed by Max were not *necessary* for thought, but were of secondary importance and merely reflected a sort of "neural overflow" from the brain and down the motor pathways. In contrast to Watson's position, with its emphasis upon *peripheral* motor activity in the thought process, this counterinterpretation of Max's data emphasizes the role of *central neural mechanisms.* These two theories, the peripheral versus the central, represent two classic approaches to the problem of thought. A definitive answer to their conflicting claims is not presently available, partly because of our limited ability to observe the complex interactions that occur in the brain. One interesting suggestion, however, amounts to a compromise between these approaches; this is the notion that during their early development, symbolic (thinking) processes may require the participation of observable peripheral systems, as suggested in Watson's theory among others. With further development, however, peripheral components tend to become less important and ultimately drop out, leaving central processes as the main mechanisms of thought. Two pieces of evidence seem pertinent here. One is the fact that Max's most intelligent subjects showed relatively little motor activity during thought, as compared to the activity levels of their duller colleagues. Secondly, children seem to place greater reliance on peripheral mechanisms than do adults; they may, for example, count on their fingers, or move their lips while reading silently.

THE WHORFIAN HYPOTHESIS

The writings of Benjamin Lee Whorf provide us with a rather different hypothesis regarding the relationship between thought and language. In essence, Whorf took the position that language largely determines the way in which we perceive and think about the world in which we live. He opposed the common-sense notion that people brought up in different language communities perceive and think about external reality in similar terms, differing only in the code (language) they use to express their thoughts. Whorf suggested that language serves as more than the passive "interpreter" or "translator" of mental life, but instead provides an all-pervasive framework that actively *contributes* to our thoughts and perceptions.

This is, of course, a strikingly relativistic doctrine. It does not merely assert that people of differing backgrounds are likely to evaluate the real world according to different norms and ethical standards; according to Whorf, the world itself—the things that seem so palpably objective and "out there"—is partly "constructed" by the linguistic habits that we have learned. Reality is different for peoples who speak different languages.

How might such a process operate? What types of language differences might we expect to affect our thoughts in this manner? Vocabulary differences have often been suggested as playing a crucial role. This is not to say that the particular sounds that a language employs are particularly important; the fact that the object from which you are now reading is called *un livre* in French, rather than *a book*, does not produce the cognitive differences Whorf had in mind. Whorf was impressed with those cases in which one language provides a rather detailed and differentiated set of labels for a given range of experience, while another language fails to differentiate these experiences (or events) and labels them all with the same word. Whorf notes, for example, that the Eskimos use three distinct words in labelling different varieties of snow, while in English these differences are glossed over. Thus, events that require three labels for the Eskimo are labelled with a single term in English: snow. This is not to suggest that English generally fails to make distinctions that are embedded in other languages. In the language of the Hopi, all flying things, with the exception of birds, are called by the same name; we regard this as an overly broad class of objects, and speak of planes, insects, kites, aviators, and so on. The languages of the world simply differ in the specificity with which they label various areas of experience; the Eskimo has a precise vocabulary for speaking about snows, while the American readily provides a specific label for the different varieties of flying objects.

How might these vocabulary differences affect our thoughts and perceptions? One possibility would be that the American is unable to distinguish between the varieties of snow that the Eskimo sees as being so very different from one another. This hardly seems likely; Whorf was apparently capable of seeing these differences, for he clearly describes the different types of snow. Similarly, it is difficult to believe that the Hopi is incapable of perceiving the difference between butterflies, airplanes, and kites. A milder version of this doctrine might assert that differences among similar things are not *automatically* detected unless the perceiver's language alerts him to the relevant distinctions. Thus, while Whorf found it possible to describe the differences between the various types of snow, it is likely that he would not normally note or attend to these differences if he was, let us say, waiting for a bus in his native city of Hartford.

Further, the distinctions captured by a *single word* in some languages may require several words, or phrases, in others. While the Eskimo has a separate single word for the different varieties of snow, the American requires many; thus, Whorf describes "snow packed hard like ice," "falling snow," and "snow on the ground." Similarly, we may surmise that with proper modifying terms the Hopi can describe the difference between various flying objects, although this may require more effort and verbiage than in English.

It is interesting to consider how Zipf's law might be applied to these observations. Recall first that, according to Zipf, the words that occur most frequently in a given language tend to be short, while the infrequent words are longer. Thus if a given event or category of experience is referred to frequently and named by a *single* word in one language (English, let us say), but is seldom referred to and requires a rather *lengthy phrase* in another language (Hopi, for instance), we may assume that for English-speaking people the event is probably of some importance. By contrast, the event is probably of lesser importance within the Hopi community. Some psychologists have gone one step further to propose that if the label for some particular event appears frequently within a given *language*, this event probably also appears quite frequently in the *thoughts* and *perceptions* of those who speak the language.

In an ingenious experiment by Brown and Lenneberg (1954), the names associated with various nonlinguistic events were shown to influence the ease with which these events could be remembered. This study, conducted with American college students, sought to demonstrate that color patches readily "coded" in English could be more readily remembered than those coded less effectively. The investigators first showed a series of colors to twenty-four students at Harvard and Radcliffe. The students were asked to name each color as quickly as they could. As you might expect, some colors, such as *red* or *blue,* could be named with little delay, while others required longer. The experimenters noted that in general the colors named quickly had *short names;* these colors also tended to elicit the *same* response when a given subject was tested twice, or when the responses of different subjects were compared. By way of contrast, the colors that could not be named immediately typically had *long* names and often failed to elicit consistent responses from one person to the next. These results suggested that one might quite meaningfully speak of the codability of the different colors—the relative ease with which they could be named. Colors that elicited short, consistent names with virtually no delay were regarded as highly codable in English.

Do these differences in codability affect the ease with which a given color might be remembered? If so, we might infer that people generally find it easier to recall events that are highly codable for them. Moreover, as we have discussed above, the events most codable in one language may not be very codable in another. If it could be demonstrated that codability affects memory, this would suggest that an event readily codable in English might be easily recalled by an American, while this same event might be recalled with greater difficulty by the speaker of some other language. In brief, the language of the memorizer would be a determinant of his cognitive behavior, as hypothesized by Whorf.

Having determined the codability of twenty-four different colors, Brown and Lenneberg next enlisted a new group of subjects who were shown four of these colors at a time. Following each presentation, the subjects were shown a collection of 120 different colors and were asked to point to the four they had just seen. As anticipated, the colors with high codability were recognized more frequently than the others. Moreover, codability had a greater effect upon recognition when a 3-minute delay was introduced between the initial exposure to the colors and the presentation of the recognition test. These results suggest that as the experimenters placed increasing demands upon their subjects' memories, the codability of the various colors became more and more important in determining whether or not they could recall what they had seen.

It is relatively easy to see how codability operated in this situation. When subjects were asked how they had remembered the various sets of color patches, they typically reported that they had tried to recall the *names* of the colors. We would, of course, expect that if a color was associated with a long descriptive name including several words, the subjects would be more likely to forget it. Moreover, since these long low-codability colors were not consistently associated with any *single* name, it might be quite difficult to select from the larger set the colors to be remembered, even if the subject succeeded in recalling the name initially "stored" in memory. In the language of general semantics, we might say that the extensional meaning (referent) for these color names was rather vague. Even if the subject could recall that he had been shown "a rather hazy combination of blue and dark green," he might have considerable difficulty in picking out the appropriate color patch. In contrast, the extensional referent for a color described as "red" would be quite clear.

More recent research by Lantz and Stefflre (1964) lends further credence to this interpretation. Using a memory-for-colors task similar to the one described above, these investigators found that the subjects' ability to communicate about a given color was an accurate predictor of the likelihood that it would be successfully recognized in the memory test. More specifically, Lantz and Stefflre devised a method for measuring communicability in which the various test colors were presented to a group of subjects who were asked to name each one in such a way that someone else would be able to pick the color out from a large set. As you might expect, some colors were simpler to communicate about than others; that is, some colors could be readily identified from the subjects' names for them, while others could not. When the various colors were later presented to a new group of subjects in a memory task, these subjects were most successful in remembering the colors that could be accurately communicated; they were less successful in remembering the colors that had presented difficulties in the communication task.

Experiments like that of Brown and Lenneberg, and of Lantz and Stefflre, demonstrate the influence of vocabulary (word-thing associations) on memory, an important form of cognitive behavior. Whorf's hypothesis concerning the linkage between language and cognition is not, however, limited to such cases. Languages differ not only in their vocabularies and in the aspects of reality that they code with greatest fidelity; they also differ in their grammatical rules. For example, the speaker of English conjugates his verbs depending upon the *time* of the action in question. In order to speak grammatically about Jack's interest in swimming, it is necessary to indicate whether he *wishes* to swim now, *wished* to swim a few days ago, or *will want* to swim tomorrow. Observe that this requires the speaker of English to take note continually of time. We may reasonably hypothesize that this characteristic of English may produce an unusual awareness and sensitivity to time; this awareness may be maintained as a generalized cognitive habit, whether we are actively speaking or not.

We should hasten to add that verbs are *not* conjugated by tense in all languages. The Wintu's language does not "force" him to distinguish past, present, and future. He must, however, choose verb forms that automatically indicate the sort of evidence that lies behind his statements. If the speaker is describing an event within his field of vision, the verb would be conjugated in one manner. If the speaker's assertion is based on hearsay, a different verb form would be required. Still another form would be used when the speaker comments on a predictable and recurrent event by asserting, for example, that "The chief is hunting" (based on knowledge that he regularly hunts at this time). These observations suggest that the speaker of Wintu may be continually forced to note the evidence that stands behind each of his statements. While it is quite clear that we too can pay close attention to this matter of evidence under appropriate conditions (when testifying at a trial, for example), the Wintu *must* do so continually and habitually in order to speak correctly.

In examining these differences between various linguistic systems, it seems quite natural to inquire about why one culture develops a finely differentiated vocabulary for labelling events in a given area while these distinctions are largely ignored in other languages. Why *does* the Eskimo have a different name for the various types of snow while we have but one? Why does our language contain such explicit information concerning the time that a given event took place, while others do not? It seems reasonable to assume that, through evolutionary changes, the language of a given community will most accurately reflect those aspects of reality concerning which exact information and communication are required. For the Eskimo, the distinctions between different snows are of critical importance, and consequently his vocabulary enables him to convey these distinctions with a minimum of effort. Similarly, this line of reasoning suggests that the importance of time within our culture was perhaps a causal factor in determining the manner in which we conjugate verbs.

Following this line of thought, it is interesting to note that, within a given culture, specialized groups often develop their own vocabularies to enable group members to speak more precisely about matters of particular concern to them. For example, clinical psychologists and psychiatrists have found it necessary to develop a specialized labelling system for referring to various forms of psychopathology. While the layman may find it quite satisfactory to use a broad term like "emotional disturbance," this label is too undifferentiated for the specialist; he develops a more precise vocabulary and speaks of manic-depressive psychosis, or passive-aggressive personality, or hebephrenic schizophrenia, to name but a few. A similar process seems to occur in informal interest groups. Note, for example, the detailed terminology of "jazz" (blues, Chicago style, bebop, funky); many of us do not find it necessary to make these distinctions, and hence we have not learned this special vocabulary.

If we grant that differences in cultural and subcultural emphasis eventually have an impact upon our language, might this be interpreted as a challenge to the Whorfian position? Does language tend to develop *in response* to cultural and cognitive factors? Or, as Whorf suggests, does language shape culture and cognition? At present it seems plausible to synthesize these conflicting approaches by hypothesizing a circular process in which the language is shaped by cultural emphasis (such as the importance of time, or the need for precise communication concerning a given domain). In turn, however, successive generations, upon learning to speak, are thereby predisposed to pay particular attention to those aspects of reality that the language reflects most faithfully and easily. Thus the American child presumably finds it easier to adjust to our emphasis upon time, since the very language that he speaks has made this an important aspect of reality.

THE REPRESENTATIONAL NATURE OF THOUGHT

Thinking often involves responding to *symbolic representations* of a problem. For example, to find the shortest route between my home and my office, I can consider the various alternatives (in my head) and then choose one *without leaving my chair*, for mechanisms of thought can represent the external environment. For some people this representational process is primarily visual—the problem situation is vividly "seen."

In addition to representing the *environment* in symbolic terms, the thought process often leads the individual to a symbolic representation of the various *action possibilities* available. Thus, in thinking about the various routes to my office, I may symbolically "try out" the available possibilities, before rendering my judgment about the shortest way. In brief, then, thinking often involves the use of symbolic processes to represent *situations* and *responses*, and may in this way be contrasted with more rudimentary trial-and-error problem-solving methods that mainly rely upon the *overt* "trying out" of various behaviors in the "real world."

Evidence for representational thought in animals. The representational capacities discussed above are not restricted to man. Available evidence indicates that some animals are also capable of representational thought. For example, in the *delayed reaction experiment,* the animal is permitted to watch as the experimenter places a food reward under one of two cups. The animal is not, however, permitted to approach either of the cups until a predetermined period has elapsed. When the animal is released, he can respond correctly only if he can somehow succeed in symbolically representing to himself (visualizing?) the earlier situation when the reward was originally placed in position. In this experiment, then, consistent success cannot be achieved by reliance on the external stimuli present during the test; success instead depends upon the animal's ability to represent past occurrences symbolically. Using this method, Hunter (1912) demonstrated wide species differences. Dogs, for example, could be delayed for 5 minutes and still respond correctly, while rats had a maximum delay of about 10 seconds. In general, the higher the phylogenetic level of the animal, the greater was its capacity for delay.

The *double alternation problem* provides another approach to the study of symbolic representation in animals. In this situation the animal is placed into a maze like the one diagrammed in Figure 21. The animal's

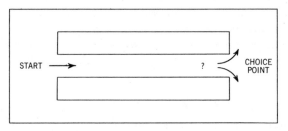

Figure 21

The double alternation problem.

task is to learn that upon reaching the choice point, the proper response depends upon his prior choices. Thus, upon approaching the choice point, the animal should first turn left; when he arrives at the choice point for the second time, he should turn left again. Having run twice around the left side of the maze, he should then shift and turn to the right on his next two choices. If he successfully executes this LLRR pattern, he will be given a reward. Note that this is a somewhat complicated procedure, for in order to respond appropriately the animal must recall (symbolically represent) his performance on the two preceding choices. If he has turned in the same direction on both of these choices, it is time for him to switch —otherwise he must repeat his most recent turn.

Results of the double alternation problem again show a systematic relationship to phylogenetic level. While the low-level rat finds the problem impossible to solve, raccoons and cats have succeeded. Continuing with this comparative trend, it is interesting to note that children who have not yet learned to speak can solve the double alternation problem although they find it quite difficult, while the task is usually rather simple for older children who are able to verbalize (Hunter and Bartlett, 1948). These last observations remind us again of the important role that language plays in problem solving. It is clear from the results of animal studies, however, that language is not a necessary skill for the successful mastery of representational problems.

REPRESENTATION OF THE FUTURE

Man's capacity to concern himself with situations beyond those that confront him in the immediate environment provides a valuable tool for everyday living. Thus, by thinking about the expenses involved in sending his children to college (even though this may be several years off), the young father may be motivated to set up a systematic savings plan. On the other hand, a person with poorly developed symbolic capacities may be primarily dependent upon the more tangible problems and rewards that immediately surround him, and may consequently find it difficult to engage in behaviors that do not yield a "pay-off" here and now. Such a person may, for example, find it difficult to complete his education, since, to continue in school, he must be willing to accept the discipline, hard work, and lack of income that go with being a student—all in the expectation that these difficulties will be more than counterbalanced by the educational, social, and financial benefits that an adequate education can provide.

Some recent research (Mischel, 1961) provides us with an interesting picture of the child mainly concerned with present rewards. In these studies, the children are first led through a series of experimental procedures (or questions), and are then thanked for their help. To reward them for their efforts, the experimenter offers them a choice between two candy bars—a *small* one available right then and there, and a *larger* candy bar the experimenter has "just run out of," but which will be given to the child on the next day if he chooses it. Using this basic technique in a study conducted on the island of Trinidad, Mischel found that juvenile delinquents were less likely to choose the larger, delayed reward than were nondelinquent youngsters. Moreover, within the delinquent group, those who did prefer the delayed reward were more socially responsible and had higher aspirations for achievement. These data indicate the systematic manner in which foresight and the capacity to delay gratification may be related to personality variables.

REPRESENTATION AS AN AID IN PROBLEM SOLVING

Man's capacity to react symbolically to his environment before engaging in *overt* behavior provides many advantages. At a very simple level, we should note the speed and minimum effort with which various solutions can be considered in thought and, if they are found wanting, discarded. In contrast, when solution attempts are enacted overtly, rather than symbolically, there may be considerable "costs" in time and effort before a given solution is proven to be inadequate. Consider, for example, someone driving home from a crowded football game. If he simply tries out the various possible routes in the order that they occur to him, he may expend considerable effort before he hits upon a satisfactory solution. He may encounter traffic jams, detoured roads, and the like in his initial attempts. By approaching this problem symbolically before putting his ideas into overt practice, he can often avoid these effortful, time-consuming, and possibly dangerous pre-solution attempts. Despite these potential advantages of the symbolic approach, we have all had experiences in which our carefully formulated plans have gone awry. In many instances this occurs when our symbolic representation of the environment is deficient in some regard. For example, in choosing a road home, we may fail to remember that the route we have selected is now being repaired. Consequently, while our choice may have seemed wise in symbolic anticipation, in actuality it may involve unexpected difficulties.

Apart from the speed, safety, and relative ease with which symbolic procedures may be applied in approaching a problem, this mode of response has still other virtues when compared with overt problem solving. Dollard and Miller (1950) point to the fact that, in the "real world," problems can only be solved by dealing *in sequence* with the various obstacles that lie between one's present position and the ultimate goal. In symbolic reasoning, on the other hand, it is possible to consider the more distant goal first, and then cast about for ways it may be reached. By reversing the normal sequence in this manner, it is sometimes possible to discover solutions to immediate problems that might otherwise prove difficult or impossible. Figure 22 provides us with a simple example.

. . . In the heavy traffic leaving a football game, a driver was caught in a long line of cars all waiting to make a left turn on a four-lane highway. . . . Most of the cars leaving the game were all waiting to make the same left turn. There was just enough traffic coming from the other direction to make the left turn difficult so the line was advancing quite

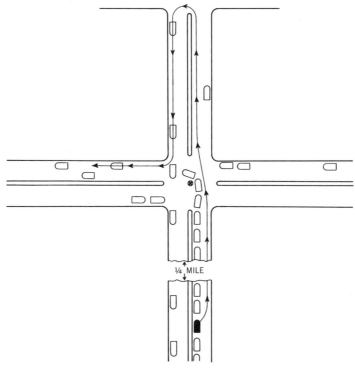

Figure 22

*Example of symbolic problem solving. (Adapted from
J. Dollard and N. E. Miller,* Personality and Psychotherapy. *New York: McGraw-Hill Book Co., Inc.,
1950.)*

slowly. Once the cars negotiated the difficult left turn, they could drive
ahead rapidly on the other highway.

As the long line of cars crept slowly ahead, the man became increasingly impatient. He wished he could pull out of the line into the almost
empty lane on the right and drive ahead. But this thought led to the one
of being stopped by the other drivers when he tried to turn left in front
of the long line so this solution was immediately rejected. The driver
continued, however, to think of the road he would like to get onto. He
noticed that the few cars coming in the opposite direction had no difficulty in making their right turns onto this road and driving rapidly on
down it. He said to himself, "If I were only going the other way, it
would be so easy." This led to the question, "How could I be going the
other way?" From here on he was dealing with a problem that he had a
great deal of practice in solving. He immediately thought of pulling out
into the outside lane, driving up the highway, finding a place to turn
around, coming back the other way, and making the right turn onto the

other highway. While thinking of this, he felt a triumphant sense of relief from the frustration of waiting in line and immediately proceeded to carry his ideas through to successful action.[1]

Note how the driver was ultimately able to arrive at a solution to his problem by first considering the fact that a right turn would be much easier to accomplish than a left turn, and then taking appropriate action based on this realization.

PROBLEM SOLVING AND THE FIXATION OF INCORRECT RESPONSES

In an earlier section we referred to the fact that successful thinking and problem solving typically involve the sudden discovery of appropriate solutions. This emphasis on discovery is important, since by definition problems typically prove to be troublesome for the simple reason that our initial and dominant reactions are likely to be incorrect—thus the solution must be discovered.

Figure 23 attempts to represent various solutions that occurred to one subject when faced with the following problem: Assume that a

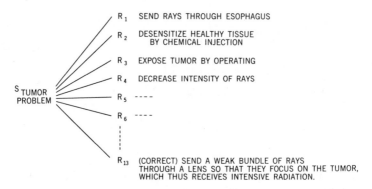

Figure 23

Diagrammatic representation of subject's successive responses to problem, based on habit-family hierarchy model.

person has an inoperable stomach tumor that can be destroyed by a ray. How can we rid our patient of the tumor without harming the healthy tissue that surrounds it, when the surrounding tissue is just as vulnerable to the ray as the tumor itself? Note that in Figure 23, which is modelled

---

[1] From J. Dollard and N. E. Miller, *Personality and Psychotherapy*. New York: McGraw-Hill Book Co., Inc., 1950. Quoted with permission of the publisher.

after Hull's habit-family hierarchy, our subject's early solutions (responses 1, 2, 3, etc.) are all inappropriate for one reason or another; in order for him to succeed, the correct solution (R_{13}) must rise to the position of dominance.

Unfortunately, people often find themselves "fixed" on an incorrect solution or approach and are unable to give it up in favor of a more appropriate response. Karl Duncker (1945), who has investigated this problem most thoroughly, suggests that this is often attributable to the individual's tendency to utilize the elements of the problem in a conventional manner that may be quite ineffective for the problem at hand. In one of his experiments, Duncker presented his subjects with the task of attaching three small candles to a door; they were given a variety of materials to help them, including some tacks, some matches, and several small match boxes. Successful solution of the problem required that the subjects tack the boxes to the door, and use them as "platforms" on which to stand the candles; to secure the candles to the boxes, they were to use the matches to melt the wax. Duncker's experiment compared the performance of two groups of subjects. For one group, the boxes were empty; for the second group, each box was filled with one of the other experimental materials (tacks, candles, or matches). The problem proved to be relatively simple when the boxes were empty—all the subjects in this group succeeded in finding the solution. In contrast, the subjects who were presented with the *filled* boxes showed much poorer performance. Duncker interprets this as indicating that the filled boxes were less likely to be perceived as miniature "platforms," as called for in the solution. The empty boxes, on the other hand, did not evoke the "container" association so strongly, which made the problem considerably easier. The main point here is that the various elements of a problem situation often have more than one use; conventional uses of an element may blind us to its other functions.

FIXATION AND DRIVE LEVEL

We are all familiar with the fact that our effectiveness as problem solvers varies. Several investigations suggest that level of motivation is an important variable. In one of these studies, Glucksberg (1962) used the match and box problem just discussed. The investigator started from a premise extensively explored in both human and animal learning: strong motivation generally results in a strengthening of the dominant responses in a habit-family hierarchy.

In Figure 24 we have depicted two habit-family hierarchies. The left diagram represents the relative strength of various responses (solutions) under low motivational conditions, while the right diagram shows the strength of these same solutions under conditions of strong motivation. The fact that the left diagram depicts responses 1, 2, 3, and 4 as being

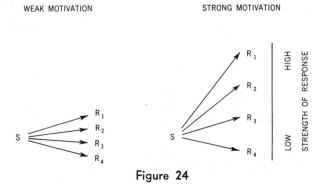

Figure 24

Effect of increased motivation on relative strengths of competing responses.

relatively close together on the vertical dimension indicates that these responses have similar (but not equal) probabilities of occurring when motive strength is low. In contrast, high motivation strengthens all four response possibilities; and most importantly for our present concerns, a high level of motivation increases the *differences* between the various responses. In effect, a dominant response like R_1 is now more likely to occur than it was before, while relatively weak responses like R_3 and R_4 will be less likely to occur, because they cannot compete as effectively with R_1.

Let us now recall that in a situation like the match and box problem, the correct solution is not likely to be initially dominant; instead, it is rather weak relative to the other responses evoked. This means that the correct response (in this case assume it is R_4), being relatively low in the hierarchy, should be even *less likely* to occur when motivation is high. That is, since increased motivation strengthens the stronger responses relative to the weaker ones, we should generally anticipate that high levels of motivation will further intensify the subject's fixation on the dominant (incorrect) response and thus impair performance. This is exactly what happened in the Glucksberg experiment. A group of subjects who had been offered a financial reward if they could solve the problem turned out to be less successful in reaching the solution than was another group that had not been promised any money.

FIXATION AND PAST EXPERIENCE

In the examples discussed above, we have tried to show how the individual's perception of the problem and the solutions that he will consider may be significantly determined by the structure of the situation that now faces him and by his level of motivation. Of course, *previous experience* may also fixate incorrect solutions to a given problem; this has been investigated most thoroughly by Luchins (1942).[2]

Table I

Problems used by Luchins (1942) in his studies of fixation. Used with permission of author.

PROBLEM	GIVEN: THE FOLLOWING EMPTY JARS AS MEASURES			OBTAIN: THE FOLLOW-ING AMOUNT OF WATER
1. (Sample)	29	3		20
2.	21	127	3	100
3.	14	163	25	99
4.	18	43	10	5
5.	9	42	6	21
6.	20	59	4	31
7.	23	49	3	20
8.	15	39	3	18
9.	28	76	3	25
10.	18	48	4	22
11.	14	36	8	6

Luchins' experiments involved the presentation of several rather simple computational problems, as shown in Table 1. The second problem in the table can be solved by (a) filling the large 127-quart jar, then (b) spilling off 21 quarts into the medium-sized jar, and finally (c) spilling off an additional 6 quarts by filling the smallest jar twice: $127 - 21 - (2 \times 3) = 100$. The experiments were constructed so that this approach could be applied to problems 2 through 6. All subsequent problems, however, could be solved in more than one way. One possibility was to follow the method that had been employed previously. Thus, in problem 7, we could obtain 20 quarts by first filling the 49-quart jar, removing 23 quarts, and then removing an additional 6 quarts by filling the 3-quart jar twice. Problem 7 and those following it could also be solved in a far simpler fashion, involving the use of only two jars; in problem 7, for example, we could get 20 quarts by simply filling the 23-quart jar and spilling off 3 quarts from it. Luchins' most important finding was that the presentation of the early problems led to a fixation on the method previously successful. The subjects' earlier successes with this method apparently prevented them from seeing that a simpler approach was possible. However, it was possible to eliminate this type of fixation if,

---

[2] This material is also presented in Luchins (1948), and in Luchins and Luchins (1959).

prior to the critical test series, the subjects were intermittently presented with problems that required *different* methods of solution.

Luchins' results seem to fit quite neatly into our earlier discussion of reinforcement, for the problem-solving responses successful in the early problems seemed to gain in strength and prevented the occurrence of the simpler solutions applicable to the test problems. Other experiments by Luchins also suggest that increases in motivation intensify the subject's fixation on the responses initially dominant in his hierarchy. In particular, Luchins found that if people were forced to solve the various water-jar problems while under time pressure, they showed increased fixation on the solution successful in the early problems. It seems plausible that the imposition of a short time limit elevated the level of motivation, which in turn strengthened the dominant responses in the individual's hierarchy.

RESTRUCTURING THE PROBLEM SITUATION

Problems are often insoluble because of our inability to discard approaches that have previously been successful. How, then, can we facilitate problem solving? One suggestion is to approach the problem from different perspectives, in the hope that the problem elements will be perceived in a new and more fruitful light. Unfortunately, it is easier to talk about this procedure than to put it into practice. We may, however, point to some clear-cut examples to see how this suggestion might work.

One good example of restructuring has to do with the manner in which a problem is stated. Difficult problems often turn out to be quite simple if they are posed appropriately. For example, consider the following: How can a person build a house so that it has southern exposure on all four sides? As stated in this form, the problem is rather difficult, yet it may be made far simpler if restated with an emphasis on *where* one might build such a house (answer: at the North Pole).

Duncker (1945) provided another example of this rewording technique. He spoke of a mountain trip on which he planned to descend from a peak by the same path he had used for the ascent on the previous day. Assuming that the ascent and descent both took place at about the same time (from five to twelve o'clock), he posed the problem of whether there must be a point that he would pass at exactly the same time of day during the ascent and descent. Stated in this form, Duncker could reach no conclusive answer. Rewording the problem, however, made the answer clear. Suppose there were *two* climbers—one at the top and one at the bottom of the mountain. If they used the same path and started at the same time, they must surely *meet* (that is, both be at the same place at the same time). Hence a single climber must pass some point at the same time of day during the course of his ascent and descent.

What are colloquially referred to as "hints" often provide another means for restructuring a problem situation. An experiment by Maier (1931) provides a good illustration. In this study, the subjects were individually led into a room that contained a variety of objects: tables, chairs, poles, pliers, and clamps. In addition, two cords hung from the ceiling to the floor—one from the center of the room and the other near a wall. The subject's task was to tie the ends of the cords together. The problem resulted from the fact that these cords were well separated, and if the subject held one in his hand, he would be unable to reach the other. One way of solving this problem was to tie a weight to the cord hanging from the center of the ceiling and then swing it like a pendulum. This would make it possible to catch the swinging cord while standing in a position near the center of the room and holding the other cord. In one experiment, subjects who were about to give up, after failing to discover this solution, were given the following hint: the experimenter merely walked about the room and, upon passing the cord hanging in the center, managed "accidentally" to put it in motion.

This hint proved relatively successful in inducing the correct solution. In explaining his results, Maier reasoned that the cord, when swaying, was more like the needed pendulum than it was when stationary. Many of these subjects commented on the suddenness with which the problem situation became reorganized. It is particularly interesting to note that these people were rarely aware of the role played by the experimenter's hint; this illustrates that problem-solving attempts may often be influenced by factors that escape our conscious deliberations.

Problems can also be restructured by varying the order in which the problem elements are considered; in this way our approach to the problem may be modified. Judson and Cofer (1956) demonstrated this in a study in which subjects were given several problems, each consisting of four words. The subject's task was to pick out the one word that was unrelated to the other three. One group, for example, included the words "subtract," "increase," "multiply," and "add." This is an ambiguous item; from one point of view we might feel that "increase" is the unrelated word, since the others all refer to some arithmetic operation. Alternatively, perhaps "subtract" is the odd word, since each of the others implies increasing magnitude. Judson and Cofer found that ambiguous items of this sort were affected by the order in which the words appeared. While "increase" was the most common response when the words were presented in the order given above, the sequence "multiply," "increase," "add," "subtract" tended to elicit "subtract" as the most common response —perhaps because of the expectations produced by the early words.

Judson and Cofer also found that their subjects' personal values and interests played a significant role in this task. Given words like "prayer," "temple," "cathedral," and "skyscraper," religious subjects were likely to respond that "skyscraper" did not belong with the other words. People without much religious interest, on the other hand, were less likely to accept the word "prayer," since to them the remaining words all appeared to have architectural referents.

This impact of attitude upon problem solving is reminiscent of an earlier section, in which we discussed the effects of attitude in the interpretation of persuasive communications. In both cases a presumably objective and rational process has been distorted by the individual's preferences. A further illustration of this process was reported by Thistlethwaite (1950). This investigator presented his subjects with several sets of logical premises concerning race relations. Their task was to select the conclusion that would logically follow from each set of premises. Note that in a task of this sort the respondent should be exclusively concerned with the logical connections between the premises he is given and the conclusion he accepts. The actual truth of a given conclusion (in the real world) and its agreement or disagreement with his own views should be irrelevant. Nevertheless, Thistlethwaite found that his respondents often tended to select conclusions consistent with their attitudes but not necessarily following from the premises.

THOUGHT AND MOTIVATION: THE THEORY OF COGNITIVE DISSONANCE

Most of the preceding material in this chapter has been concerned with the adaptive significance of thought, and with the various factors that determine its character and effectiveness. Despite the importance of these concerns, we should not overlook the role of thought as a motivator for further action. Festinger's theory of cognitive dissonance (1957), which deals with the motivating effects of "nonfitting" or dissonant cognitive elements, provides a good example. Festinger's main hypothesis is that the simultaneous presence of two or more dissonant cognitions (or ideas) results in a noxious drive state that people will attempt to resolve.

For example, a student opposed to cheating would not normally engage in this form of behavior. If this person *does* cheat, we might expect that this action will place him in a state of dissonance, since his initial attitude toward cheating would be clearly inconsistent with the knowledge that he has cheated. The theory of cognitive dissonance leads to the expectation that our cheating student will probably become more lenient in his views toward cheating, since this would reduce the discrepancy between his past actions and his present attitudes. In contrast, a student who has had the opportunity to cheat but does not do so should become even more severely opposed to cheating, for an attitude of severe condemnation would be most consistent with this resistance to temptation. An experiment by Mills (1958) verified these predictions.

Festinger and his colleagues have carefully examined other situations in which an individual's actions do *not* follow from his private beliefs.

For example, eighth-grade children induced to eat vegetables they previously disliked will generally come to regard these foods more positively (Brehm, 1959). According to dissonance theory, this result is obtained because of the inconsistency (dissonance) between the individual's initially negative attitude toward a given vegetable, and the knowledge that he has just eaten this particular food. However, this dissonance can be resolved, and the associated tension reduced, if the child changes his views about the vegetable in question.

In other tests of dissonance theory, surprising results have sometimes been reported. For example, in one experiment (Cohen, Brehm, and Fleming, 1958), two groups of Yale students were induced to write essays that opposed their private views on a change to coeducational classes at that all-male institution. One group was given little justification for writing their essays, while the other was given more detailed and emphatic reasons. Surprisingly, the essay-writing experience led the subjects who were given *little* justification to change their private attitudes more markedly than those given more extensive justification. These data fit the dissonance formulation if we make the reasonable assumption that when people with scant external justification write essays that depart from their private views, they probably experience more dissonance than those who *are* given adequate justification for engaging in this discrepant behavior. Given the greater dissonance in the "low justification" group, we should anticipate more attitude change as subjects make their private views more congruent with their written statements.

The theory of cognitive dissonance has stimulated experimentation in a variety of fields and has led to a wider appreciation of the importance of cognitive inconsistency as a determinant and motivator of human behavior.

SUMMARY

1. Psychologists have long been concerned with the distinction between thinking and learning. Thorndike argued that in problem solving he could see little evidence of insight; rather, he emphasized the importance of trial-and-error behavior plus the law of effect. Köhler, on the other hand, felt that problem solving could not be reduced to these simple concepts. He contended that insight, based on the perceptual reorganization of problem elements, played a crucial role.

2. Harlow's research on learning sets provides evidence concerning the importance of earlier trial-and-error experience for the development of insight. In his studies, he demonstrated that animals "learn to learn" and gradually progress from a stage in which their problem-solving efforts are characterized by *gradual* improvement, much as suggested by Thorndike's law-of-effect theory. With further problem-solving experience, animals gradually become more skillful at such tasks until they are

ultimately capable of showing insightful behavior in response to new problems.

3. Watson theorized that thinking is similar to speaking but without overt expression; thus, he regarded thought as implicit or subvocal speech.

4. According to Benjamin Whorf, language and thought are quite closely related in the sense that language provides the basic framework on which thought is constructed. This view assumes that people with different linguistic backgrounds are likely to think about and perceive the world in rather different ways.

5. In thinking, it is often necessary for us symbolically to represent the various elements of the problem with which we are dealing. However, this ability is not restricted to man; it can be demonstrated in animals as well.

6. Attempts at problem solving are often unsuccessful because of the individual's tendency to become fixated on some incorrect solution or approach. Karl Duncker theorized that this is usually attributable to the fact that various problem elements may be perceived in a conventional manner quite ineffective for the problem at hand. This type of fixation is most likely to occur when the individual is highly motivated.

7. Festinger's theory of cognitive dissonance is based on the idea that the simultaneous presence of two or more "nonfitting" ideas leads to a noxious state that will motivate the individual to reduce this dissonance. Many supporting experiments have been conducted—for example, some showing that if people can be induced (without much external pressure) to behave in ways that conflict with their own private beliefs, they will often change their views to make them more consistent with the actions they have displayed.

CREATIVITY

How can we account for the genius of Leonardo Da Vinci? How can we increase the creativity of our children? Questions like these have been asked with increasing frequency as psychologists and educators have worked to unravel the origins of creativity.

Although many people believe that creativity is simply one aspect of intelligence, this view has been severely questioned in recent years. While it is undeniable that outstanding creative accomplishments demand above-average intelligence, creativity is not the same thing as intelligence measured in the typical IQ test. As often noted, traditional intelligence tests with questions having only one "correct" answer may penalize someone who approaches his task in a novel way. Moreover, intelligence tests place considerable emphasis upon the individual's ability to recall items he has learned in the past (definitions of words, for example), but do not give him an opportunity to demonstrate his originality or inventiveness. Thus, while there is some evidence that people high in intelligence are more likely to be creative than those who are relatively dull, extremely intelligent people do not necessarily excel in creative activities.

One of the main factors that seems important in creativity is the ability to see things in an original way. People we honor for their contributions to art, literature, and science have generally approached their work in an inventive and novel manner. We should hasten to add, however, that originality is not the only ingredient in the makeup of the creative man. After all, an original solution to a problem may be novel but may ultimately turn out to be worthless. For example, while I may be the first homeowner on my block to think of fertilizing the lawn with shaving cream, this original idea would not qualify as a creative act, since it would hardly prove to be a worthwhile plan in the long run. Similarly, while paranoid schizophrenics may sometimes give original and inventive accounts for various phenomena ("Congealed blood is an essential ingredient in the production of India ink"), we hesitate to classify these unique and eccentric utterances as evidence of creative ability because of their shortcomings when evaluated by the community at large. Creativity, then, demands more than just originality; a creative act also fits some worthwhile purpose.

One way to study the creative process is to find out all that we can about people who have shown unusual creativity. How might we select such a group? One technique is to have experts in various fields select the most creative members of their professions. When we have identified such a gifted group, we may then compare them with a less distinguished group drawn from the same occupation. We may, for example, compare creative scientists and their less creative scientific colleagues.

A series of studies following this general approach has been conducted at the University of California in Berkeley (Barron, 1965). The general plan was to invite selected individuals from such areas as mathematics, creative writing, and architecture to participate in an extensive three-day assessment procedure. During the assessment, the participants lived in a former fraternity house on the Berkeley campus and interacted with the assessment staff in a rather open social relationship. The participants also completed a variety of personality tests to elucidate further their individual characteristics.

The assessment staff found that the creative people were relatively unconventional and individualistic; they were also felt to be somewhat self-centered and moody. This emphasis on individuality and self-centeredness was also revealed in other results showing that creative people are likely to be particularly steadfast in maintaining their independence of judgment in situations where they find themselves at odds with those around them. The fact that creative people are often individualistic and independent should not surprise us; after all, truly creative work is characterized in part by its distinctiveness and originality. The scientist or writer who was unduly sensitive to the opinions of others would doubtless find it difficult to initiate successful innovations.

How about the psychological health of the creative person? Some people have felt that creative writers and scientists tend to be a bit disturbed (the stereotyped "mad scientist" is particularly pertinent here). The findings of the California studies are rather complex in this regard. One measure of psychopathology is the Minnesota Multiphasic Personality Inventory (MMPI), which enables us to compare the individual's test responses with those of people previously diagnosed as suffering from various psychological maladies, such as hypochondriasis, depression, hysteria, etc. On this test, outstanding creative writers showed consistently more evidence of psychopathology than did writers who were less eminent; similar findings were reported in a study of creative architects.

Despite these MMPI results, the creative person cannot simply be described as more disturbed than average, for his effective achievements are inconsistent with this view. Moreover, other test findings show the creative individual in a more favorable light than his less creative colleagues. For example, in the Berkeley studies, the more creative people tended to be high in self-acceptance, flexibility, and the ability to achieve through independence (rather than conformance). They were also significantly lower than the general population on a scale that assessed the individual's "effort to make a good impression." These findings point to the creative person's psychological strengths and his tendency to rely on his *own* resources.

One finding that may surprise you in these studies is the fact that, in certain respects, the creative scientist resembled the artist. This similarity was most strikingly revealed on a test measuring the individual's liking for complex and asymmetric forms, as opposed to forms that are simple, balanced, and regular. In this test, the individual was given a series of line drawings to separate into two groups: those that he liked and those that he disliked. Early research indicated that artists had a strong preference for complex and asymmetric figures, while the average person was likely to prefer designs that were more regular and balanced. More recent work with this test indicates that a preference for complexity is also characteristic of creative scientists, writers, and architects. Frank Barron, a most active investigator in this area, theorizes that the creative person may be more at home with disorder and complexity, partly because of his ready acceptance of the unconscious aspects of himself, which also partake of turbulence and instability. Presumably these unconscious origins, rather than logic and rationality, are the source of the creative impulse.

AGE AND CREATIVITY

For several decades psychologists have been interested in the effect of age upon various aspects of human behavior. Thus studies have shown the relationship between age and reaction time, age and intellectual performance, and, quite recently, between age and creative performance. In what is doubtless the most extensive study in this domain, Lehman (1953) has investigated the ages when men of various professions are most likely to make superior contributions to their fields. Table 2 summarizes his findings. As you can see, Lehman's results suggest that the most highly regarded creative contributions are usually produced by men between the ages of 30 and 40. This association between youth and creativity is particularly marked in the sciences. It is also interesting to note that in most fields the gifted contributor not only produces his *best work* at a relatively early age, but is also *most productive* (in terms of the total number of works produced) during these same early years.

Despite the striking consistency of Lehman's results in a variety of creative areas, we can only speculate at the underlying factors that produced them. One possibility may simply have to do with the individual's acceptance of the prevalent views and approaches in his field; the older man may more likely be steeped in traditional methods and find it difficult to conceive of a truly original and creative approach.

Another way of interpreting these data emphasizes the fact that age differences are probably associated with differences in sheer energy out-

Table 2

Ages at which Lehman found maximum rate of very superior contributions in different fields. (From Introduction to Psychology, 3rd edition, by Ernest R. Hilgard, copyright © 1953, 1957, 1963 by Harcourt, Brace & World, Inc., and reproduced with their permission. Data from Lehman, 1953.)

GENERAL FIELD OF CREATIVE WORK	AGE AT TIME OF MAXIMUM RATE OF CONTRIBUTION			
	25–30	30–35	35–40	40–45
Physical sciences, mathematics, inventions	Chemistry	Mathematics Physics Electronics Practical inventions Surgical techniques	Geology Astronomy	
Biological sciences and medicine		Botany Classical descriptions of disease	Bacteriology Physiology Pathology Medical discoveries	
		Genetics Entomology Psychology		
Philosophy, education, and social sciences		Economics and political science		
			Logic Ethics Esthetics "General philosophy" Educational theory and practice	Metaphysics
			Social philosophy	
Musical compositions	Instrumental selections	Vocal solos Symphonies	Chamber music Nonsymphonic orchestral music Grand opera	Cantatas Light opera and musical comedy
Literary compositions	Lyrics and ballads (German) Odes Elegies Pastoral poetry Narrative poetry Sonnets Lyric poetry	Satiric poetry Short stories Religious poetry (hymns) Comedies	Tragedies "Most influential books" Hymns by women	Novels "Best books" Best sellers Miscellaneous prose writings
Painting and sculpture		Oil paintings	American sculpture	Modern architecture Oil paintings (contemporary artists)

put. Thus it seems possible that a young man's creativity may be related to his high energy level and his high resultant rate of production. The main point here is that the young person demonstrably produces *more* than his older colleagues (perhaps because of his more abundant energy level). Having created many works, the youthful contributor is thus more likely to produce an *outstanding* contribution than is his less productive older colleague. Note that this line of argument leads to the further expectation that, regardless of age, the more productive an individual is (in terms of number of contributions), the more likely he is to create a work of outstanding significance. This expectation is, indeed, borne out by the facts, for it is clear that in virtually all fields of intellectual endeavor, the eminent workers tend to produce more works than their less distinguished colleagues. While it is probably true that a man's sheer productivity (apart from the *quality* of his work) may be an important factor in establishing his eminence, this line of approach does not seem completely satisfactory. There remains the possibility that the creative individual may have more ideas and more energy to carry them out than his less creative colleagues.

STIMULATING CREATIVITY IN GROUPS

It is widely agreed that creativity is often limited by the individual's inability to divorce himself from the traditional approaches to the problem with which he is faced. In some instances, this inability may be attributed to the individual's fear that what he perceives as a fresh and possibly promising approach may be dismissed by others as silly and worthless. Under these circumstances, creative ideas will frequently be suppressed and not voiced publicly. Indeed, we may anticipate that after repeated suppressions of this sort, the individual may ultimately find it difficult to generate truly original proposals even in the privacy of his own thought.

To escape from this dilemma, some investigators (Osborn, 1953) have suggested the use of "brain-storming" sessions in which the members of a group are encouraged to offer possible solutions to a problem, with particular emphasis on *production* of new ideas, rather than on their *evaluation*. It is hoped that in this type of permissive atmosphere the group will benefit from the individual's freedom to explore "way-out" possibilities that might otherwise be quickly rejected as too hare-brained or never offered at all. Only after the conclusion of this idea-finding stage is the group encouraged to consider the "goodness" of the various proposals. This approach to problem solving, with its heavy emphasis upon *deferred judgment* (postponing the evaluation of ideas until a large number have been collected), has also been adapted to the *individual* thinker. In this case, the problem solver is instructed to reserve all judgments about the value of his tentative solutions until he has completed an initial period of idea finding.

Unfortunately, despite the wide publicity that these brain-storming methods have received, and the very reasonable theoretical basis on which they were formulated, there is at present only scant supporting evidence for the brain-storming approach to creative problem solving. In one study, for example, the brain-storming method failed to produce any more original ideas than were generated by individuals working alone (Taylor et al., 1958).

N. R. F. Maier (1962) suggests that problem-solving conferences can be made more effective if the group leader emphasizes problem-mindedness, rather than solution-mindedness. This suggestion derives from the fact that the average group member strives too quickly for a solution—often before agreement has been reached about the nature of the problem with which the group is faced. Maier also stresses the importance of having a group leader who will encourage diversity of opinion and protect minority views, since creative ideas often come from these origins. Recent laboratory studies indicate that when personalities of group members are diverse, the group often solves problems more effectively (Hoffman and Maier, 1961)—probably because a group composed of diverse individuals is likely to consider many more distinct solution possibilities than is a group with members similar to one another.

STIMULATING ORIGINALITY

Maltzman and his co-workers (1960) offer another approach to the problem of conformist, stereotyped thinking. These investigators attempted to increase the individual's capacity to respond in original ways to word-association tests and to a somewhat related task in the Unusual Uses test, in which subjects are instructed to list unusual uses for such everyday objects as a newspaper or a brick. In both kinds of tests, originality of response was determined by comparing the individual's answers with those of others. People who gave unusual word associations, or who listed object uses that did not commonly appear, were regarded as original.

The experimenters took the position that originality in these test situations might be enhanced if the subjects were first reinforced for showing original behavior in some other context. The assumption was that the reinforcement of original responses in a preliminary *training session* would indirectly strengthen *other* original responses through response generalization (see p. 39), and this indirect strengthening would presumably be reflected in the word-association and Unusual Uses test. To investigate this hypothesis, Maltzman et al. developed a procedure in which subjects were first administered a word-association test in an unusual manner: the same stimulus words were presented six different times, and subjects were instructed to give a different response on each repetition. In this way, subjects were forced to go beyond the common associations to the stimulus words and were induced to respond in a more original manner. Following this training procedure, they were presented with a final word-association test (just once, in the usual manner) and with the Unusual Uses test. The results indicated that the training procedure did in fact enhance the originality of subjects' responses on these last two tests (as compared with control subjects). While these results do not deal with creativity—since creativity is more than originality—they do suggest an interesting approach to the problem of stereotyped, conformist thinking.

CREATIVITY AS THE FORMATION OF NEW ASSOCIATIVE LINKAGES

Many students of creativity have commented upon the fact that creative productions often seem to result from a novel combination of elements previously disconnected. Creativity in scientific fields often takes this form and is perhaps best exemplified where a scientist formulates a new theory that encompasses several diverse phenomena. For example, Einstein's general field theory was able to account successfully for observations in widely scattered areas. Similarly, creative productions in art and literature often appear to result from an original combination of distinct elements that had not previously been brought together.

Starting with this essential notion, Mednick (1964) has developed an experimental method for assessing creativity called the remote associates test (RAT). In this test, the subject is presented with three unrelated words such as "rat, blue, and cottage" and is asked to think of a word that might serve as a single connective link for the three. In this example, the response "cheese" would be scored as correct, since it is in fact associated with all three stimulus elements. The RAT consists of many items of this general type, all constructed with a view to seeing if the subject can succeed in finding a single response word associated with three rather distinct stimulus elements. Early work with the RAT has yielded some promising results, but much remains to be learned in the expanding field of research on creativity.

SUMMARY

1. Creativity should not be confused with high intelligence, for the typical IQ test does not assess originality or inventiveness. However, there is some association between intelligence and creativity.

2. We should also be careful to distinguish between creativity and originality. An idea that is original in the sense that no one else may think of it may ultimately prove to be worthless. Creativity is thus more than originality; a creative act must also serve some worthwhile purpose.

3. Creative people are often somewhat unconventional and indi-

vidualistic. They also seem to prefer complex, asymmetric drawings, rather than more balanced and regular designs. This preference for complex designs is characteristic not only of creative artists, but also of creative writers, scientists, and architects.

4. Outstanding creative works are usually produced by relatively young people; this finding appears in many fields and particularly in the sciences.

5. "Brain-storming" sessions represent an attempt to overcome traditional approaches to a problem by encouraging the members of a group to focus first upon the *production* of new ideas before evaluating the various suggestions offered. It is hoped that this permissive atmosphere will encourage the exploration of original possibilities that might otherwise be rejected as silly or worthless. Unfortunately, at present there is no really good evidence to support the optimistic claims voiced in behalf of the brain-storming technique.

6. Creative productions often seem to result from a novel combination of elements previously not connected. This form of creativity is particularly pertinent in scientific fields, where a new theory may encompass several seemingly diverse phenomena. Mednick has developed a remote associates test (RAT) in which the individual attempts to provide a single verbal response associated with each of three unrelated stimulus words.

REFERENCES

Ager, J. W., and Dawes, R. M.   The effect of judges' attitudes on judgment. *J. pers. soc. Psychol.*, 1965, *1*, 533–538.

Alter, M., and Silverman, R. E.   The response in programmed instruction. *J. Programed Instruction*, 1962, *1*, 55–78.

Ammons, R. B.   Effects of knowledge on performance: A survey and tentative theoretical formulation. *J. gen. Psychol.*, 1956, *54*, 279–299.

Barron, F.   The psychology of creativity. In Newcomb, T. M. (Ed.), *New directions in psychology II*. New York: Holt, 1965.

Bartlett, F. C.   *Remembering: A study in experimental and social psychology.* Cambridge, Eng.: Cambridge Univ. Press, 1932.

Berkowitz, L., and Goranson, R. E. Motivational and judgmental determinants of social perception. *J. abnorm. soc. Psychol.*, 1964, *69*, 296–302.

Birch, H. G.   The relation of previous experience to insightful problem-solving. *J. comp. Psychol.*, 1945, *38*, 367–383.

Blodgett, H. C.   The effect of the introduction of reward upon the maze performance of rats. *Univ. Calif. Publ. Psychol.*, 1929, *4*, 113–134.

Blum, G. S.   *Psychodynamics: The science of unconscious mental forces.* Belmont, Calif.: Wadsworth, 1966.

Bousfield, W. A.   The occurrence of clustering in the recall of randomly arranged associates. *J. gen. Psychol.*, 1953, *49*, 229–240.

Bower, G., and Trabasso, T.   Reversals prior to solution in concept identification. *J. exp. Psychol.*, 1963, *66*, 409–418.

Brookshire, K. H., Warren, J. M., and Ball, G. G.   Reversal and transfer learning following overtraining in rat and chicken. *J. comp. Psychol.*, 1961, *54*, 98–102.

Brown, R. W., and Lenneberg, E. H.   A study in language and cognition. *J. abnorm. soc. Psychol.*, 1954, *49*, 454–462.

Bruner, J. S., Goodnow, J. J., and Austin, G. A.   *A study of thinking*. New York: Science Editions, Inc., 1962.

Burtt, H. E.   An experimental study of early childhood memory. *J. gen. Psychol.*, 1941, *58*, 435–439.

Carmichael, L., Hogan, H. P., and Walter, A. A.   An experimental study of the effect of language on the reproduction of visually perceived forms. *J. exp. Psychol.*, 1932, *15*, 73–86.

Cliff, N.   Adverbs as multipliers. *Psychol. Rev.*, 1959, *66*, 27–44.

Cohen, A. R., Brehm, J. W., and Fleming, W. H. Attitude change and justification for compliance. *J. abnorm. soc. Psychol.*, 1958, *56*, 276–278.

Cohen, B. D., Kalish, H. I., Thruston, J. R., and Cohen, E. Experimental manipulation of verbal behavior. *J. exp. Psychol.*, 1954, *47*, 106–110.

Cohen, I. Programed learning and the Socratic dialogue. *Amer. Psychologist*, 1962, *17*, 772–775.

Deese, J. *The psychology of learning.* New York: McGraw-Hill, 1958.

Dollard, J., and Miller, N. E. *Personality and psychotherapy.* New York: McGraw-Hill, 1950.

Duncker, K. On problem solving. (Trans. from 1935 original.) *Psychol. Monogr.*, 1945, *58*, No. 270.

Ebbinghaus, H. *Memory.* Trans. by H. A. Ruges and C. E. Bussenius. New York: Columbia Univ. Press, 1913.

Edwards, A. L. Political frames of reference as a factor influencing recognition. *J. abnorm. soc. Psychol.*, 1941, *36*, 34–50.

Festinger, L. *A theory of cognitive dissonance.* Stanford, Calif.: Stanford Univ. Press, 1957.

Glanzer, M., and Clark, W. H. Accuracy of perceptual recall: An analysis of organization. *J. verb. Learning and verb. Behav.*, 1963, *1*, 289–299.

Glucksberg, S. The influence of strength of drive on functional fixedness and perceptual recognition. *J. exp. Psychol.*, 1962, *63*, 36–41.

Goldstein, L. S., and Gotkin, L. G. A review of research: Teaching machines vs. programed textbooks as presentation models. *J. Programed Instruction*, 1962, *1*, 29–42.

Gormezano, I., and Grant, D. A. Progressive ambiguity in the attainment of concepts on the Wisconsin card sorting test. *J. exp. Psychol.*, 1958, *55*, 621–627.

Greenspoon, J. The reinforcing effect of two spoken sounds on the frequency of two responses. *Amer. J. Psychol.*, 1955, *68*, 409–416.

Grice, G. R. The relation of secondary reinforcement to delayed reward in visual discrimination learning. *J. exp. Psychol.*, 1948, *38*, 1–16.

Guthrie, E. R., and Horton, G. P. *Cats in a puzzle box.* New York: Rinehart, 1946.

Harlow, H. F. The formation of learning sets. *Psychol. Rev.*, 1949, *56*, 51–65.

Herman, D. T., Lawless, R. H., and Marshall, R. W. Variables in the effect of language on the reproduction of visually perceived forms. *Percept. mot. Skills, Monogr. Suppl. 2*, 1957, *7*, 171–186.

Hilgard, E. R. *Introduction to psychology.* (3rd ed.) New York: Harcourt, 1962.

Hoffman, L. R., and Maier, N. R. F. Quality and acceptance of problem solutions by members of homogeneous and heterogeneous groups. *J. abnorm. soc. Psychol.*, 1961, *62*, 401–407.

Hovland, C. I., Harvey, O. J., and Sherif, M. Assimilation and contrast effects in reaction to communication and attitude change. *J. abnorm. soc. Psychol.*, 1957, *55*, 244–252.

Howe, E. S. Probabilistic adverbial qualifications of adjectives. *J. verb. Learning and verb. Behav.*, 1963, *1*, 225–242.

Hull, C. L. Quantitative aspects of the evolution of concepts. *Psychol. Monogr.*, 1920, No. 123.

Hunter, W. S. The delayed reaction in animals and children. *Animal Behav. Monogr.*, 1912, *2*, No. 1.

Jenkins, J. G., and Dallenbach, K. M. Obliviscence during sleep and waking. *Amer. J. Psychol.*, 1924, *35*, 605–612.

Johnson, W. *People in quandaries.* New York: Harper, 1946.

Judson, A. I., and Cofer, C. N. Reasoning as an associative process: I. "Direction" in a simple verbal problem. *Psychol. Rep.*, 1956, *2*, 469–476.

Katona, G. *Organizing and memorizing.* New York: Columbia Univ. Press, 1940.

Kendler, H. H., and D'Amato, M. F. A comparison of reversal and nonreversal shifts in human concept formation behavior. *J. exp. Psychol.*, 1955, *49*, 165–174.

Kendler, T. S. Verbalization and optional reversal shifts among kindergarten children. *J. verb. Learning and verb. Behav.*, 1964, *3*, 428–436.

————, and Kendler, H. H. Reversal and nonreversal shifts in kindergarten children. *J. exp. Psychol.*, 1959, *58*, 56–60.

Köhler, W. *The mentality of apes.* New York: Harcourt, 1925.

Korzybski, A. *Science and sanity.* Lancaster, Pa.: Science Press, 1933.

Lambert, W. E., and Jacobovits, L. A. Verbal satiation and changes in the intensity of meaning. *J. exp. Psychol.*, 1960, *60*, 376–383.

Lane, H., and Bem, D. A. *Laboratory manual for the control and analysis of behavior.* Belmont, Calif.: Wadsworth, 1965.

Lantz, D., and Stefflre, V. Language and cognition revisited. *J. abnorm. soc. Psychol.*, 1964, *69*, 472–481.

Lehman, H. C. *Age and achievement.* Princeton, N.J.: Princeton Univ. Press, 1953.

Lewis, H. B., and Franklin, M. An experimental study of the role of the ego in work: II. The significance of task orientation in work. *J. exp. Psychol.*, 1944, *34*, 195–215.

Lorge, I., and Thorndike, E. L. The influence of delay in the aftereffect of a connection. *J. exp. Psychol.*, 1935, *18*, 186–194.

Luchins, A. S. Mechanization in problem solving: The effect of *Einstellung. Psychol. Monogr.*, 1942, *54*, No. 248.

————. *Examination of rigidity of behavior.* New York: N.Y.R.O. Veterans Administration, 1948.

————, and Luchins, E. S. *Rigidity of behavior; a variational approach to the effect of* Einstellung. Eugene, Ore.: Univ. of Oregon Books, 1959.

Maier, N. R. F. Reasoning in white rats. *Comp. Psychol. Monogr.*, 1929, *6*, No. 29.

——————. Reasoning in humans: II. The solution of a problem and its appearance in consciousness. *J. comp. Psychol.*, 1931, *12*, 181–194.

——————. Leadership principle for problem solving conferences. *Mich. Bus. Rev.*, *14*, No. 3.

Maltzman, I. On the training of originality. *Psychol. Rev.*, 1960, *67*, 229–242.

Manis, M. The interpretation of opinion statements as a function of message ambiguity and recipient attitude. *J. abnorm. soc. Psychol.*, 1961, *63*, 76–81(a).

——————. The interpretation of opinion statements as a function of recipient attitude and source prestige. *J. abnorm. soc. Psychol.*, 1961, *63*, 82–86(b).

——————, Gleason, T. G., and Dawes, R. M. The evaluation of complex social stimuli. *J. pers. soc. Psychol.* (in press).

Mednick, S. A. The associative basis of the creative process. *Psychol. Rev.*, 1962, *69*, 220–228.

Miller, G. A. *Language and communication.* New York: McGraw-Hill, 1951.

——————. Psycholinguistics. In Lindzey, G., *A handbook of social psychology.* Cambridge, Mass.: Addison-Wesley, 1954.

——————. The magical number seven; plus or minus two: Some limits on our capacity for processing information. *Psychol. Rev.*, 1956, *63*, 81–97.

——————. The psycholinguistics. *Encounter*, 1964, *18*, No. 1, 29–40.

——————, and Selfridge, J. A. Verbal context and recall of meaningful material. *Amer. J. Psychol.*, 1950, *63*, 176–185.

——————, Heise, G. A., and Lichter, W. The intelligibility of speech as a function of the context of the test materials. *J. exp. Psychol.*, 1951, *41*, 329–335.

Mills, J. Changes in moral attitudes follow temptation. *J. Pers.*, 1958, *26*, 517–531.

Mischel, W. Preference for delayed reward and social responsibility. *J. abnorm. soc. Psychol.*, 1961, *62*, 1–7.

Osborn, A. F. *Applied imagination.* New York: Scribner's, 1953.

Osgood, C. E. *Method and theory in experimental psychology.* New York: Oxford Univ. Press, Inc., 1953.

——————, Suci, G., and Tannenbaum, P. *The measurement of meaning.* Urbana, Ill.: The Univ. of Illinois Press, 1957.

Osler, S. F., and Fivel, M. W. Concept attainment: I. The role of age and intelligence in concept attainment by induction. *J. exp. Psychol.*, 1961, *62*, 1–8(a).

——————, and Trautman, G. E. Concept attainment: II. Effect of stimulus complexity upon concept attainment at two levels of intelligence. *J. exp. Psychol.*, 1961, *62*, 9–13(b).

Postman, L., and Adams, P. A. Performance variables in the experimental analysis of the law of effect. *Amer. J. Psychol.*, 1954, *67*, 612–631.

Rosenzweig, S. An experimental study of "repression" with special reference to need-persistive and ego-defensive reactions to frustration. *J. exp. Psychol.*, 1943, *32*, 64–74.

Sapir, E. Time perspective in aboriginal American culture: A study in method. *Geological Survey, Department of Mines*, Canada, Memoir 90, No. 13, Anthropological series, 1916, *62*, 54–57.

Skinner, B. F. *Verbal behavior.* New York: Appleton-Century-Crofts, Inc., 1957.

——————. Teaching machines. *Science*, 1958, *128*, 969–977.

Spielberger, C. D. The role of awareness in verbal conditioning. *J. Pers.*, 1962, *30*, 73–101.

Stagner, R. The redintegration of pleasant and unpleasant experience. *Amer. J. Psychol.*, 1931, *43*, 463–468.

Taylor, D. W., Berry, P. C., and Block, C. H. Does group participation when using brainstorming facilitate or inhibit creative thinking? *Admin. Sci. Quart.*, 1958, *3*, 23–47.

Taylor, W. L. "Cloze procedure": A new tool for measuring readability. *Journ. Quart.*, 1953, *30*, 415–433.

Thistlethwaite, D. Attitude and structure as factors in the distortion of reasoning. *J. abnorm. soc. Psychol.*, 1950, *45*, 442–458.

Thorndike, E. L. *The fundamentals of learning.* New York: Teach. Coll., 1932.

——————. Animal intelligence. *Psychol. Monogr.*, 1898, *2*, No. 8.

Underwood, B. J. Interference and forgetting. *Psychol. Rev.*, 1957, *64*, 49–60.

——————, and Hughes, R. H. Gradients of generalized verbal responses. *Amer. J. Psychol.*, 1950, *63*, 422–430.

Walker, E. L. *Conditioning and instrumental learning.* Belmont, Calif.: Wadsworth, 1966.

Ward, C. D. Ego involvement and the absolute judgment of attitude statements. *J. pers. soc. Psychol.*, 1965, *2*, 202–208.

Woodworth, R. S. *Experimental psychology.* New York: Holt, 1938.

Zeigarnik, B. III. Das Behalten er lediger und unerledigter Handlungen. In Lewin, K. (Ed.), Untersuchungen zur Handlungs—und Affecktpsychologie. *Psychol. Forsch.*, 1927, *9*, 1–85.

Zeller, A. F. An experimental analogue of repression: II. The effect of individual failure and success on memory measured by relearning. *J. exp. Psychol.*, 1950, *40*, 411–422.

Zipf, G. K. *Human behavior and the principle of least effort.* Cambridge, Mass.: Addison-Wesley, 1949.

INDEX

Abstraction, 41–42
Adams, P. A., 10, 116
Ager, J. W., 77, 113
Alter, M., 14, 114
Ammons, R. B., 9, 113
Assign learning, 60
Assimilation effect, 72–75, 79
Associations:
    remote, 111–112
    and semantic differential, 61, 78
Attitude:
    and logic, 102
    and memory, 32
    and message interpretation, 72–79
Austin, G. A., 54, 113
Awareness:
    and concept formation, 46
    and reinforcement, 11–12

Barron, F., 106, 113
Bartlett, F. C., 24, 93, 113
Bem, D. A., 13, 21, 115
Berkowitz, L., 76, 113
Birch, H. G., 83, 113
Blodgett, H. C., 7–8, 113
Bower, G., 49, 113
Brain damage, 42–43
Brainstorming, 109–110, 112
Brehm, J., 103, 113
Brown, R. W., 88–89, 113
Bruner, J. S., 54, 113
Burtt, H. E., 19, 113

Carmichael, L., 25, 113
Category:
    and concept formation, 44
    conjunctive, 45, 54
    disjunctive, 45, 54
    relational, 45–46, 54
Clark, W. H., 23–24, 114
Cliff, N., 63, 113
Closure, 26
Cloze technique, 69
Codability and memory, 88–89
Coding and memory, 22–24
Cofer, C. N., 101, 115
Cognitive dissonance, 102–104
Cohen, A. R., 103, 113
Cohen, B. B., 56, 113
Cohen, E., 56, 113
Cohen, I., 14, 114
Common sense, 1
Compound stimuli, 62–63
Comprehensible writing, 69
Concept:
    conjunctive, 45–46, 54

Concept (continued)
    disjunctive, 45, 54
    formation, 44–45
        strategies of, 52–54, 55
    relational, 45–46, 55
    on semantic differential, 61
Concreteness, 41–42
Conditioning, 59
Connotative meaning, 60–62
Continuity versus discontinuity in concept formation, 47–51, 55
Consensual validation, 71, 76, 79
Contrast effect, 72–76, 79
Control of verbal behavior, 57–58
Creative persons, characteristics, 106–109, 111–112
Creativity, 105–112
    and age, 107–109
    and intelligence, 105
    and originality, 105, 111
    and psychological health, 106
    and remote associations, 111
    stimulating creativity, 109–110

Da Vinci, L., 105
Dallenbach, K. M., 27–28, 115
Dawes, R. M., 62, 77, 113, 116
Deese, J., 7, 29, 114
Delay of feedback, 9–10, 16
    and programmed learning, 13
Delayed reaction experiment, 92
Denotative meaning, 60–61
Discrimination training, 40, 87
Discriminative stimulus, 56–57
Dollard, J., 94–95, 114
Double alternation problem, 92
Duncker, K., 100, 104, 114

Ebbinghaus, H., 18–20, 30, 33, 114
Edwards, A. L., 32, 114
Experimental extinction, 6
    and memory, 19
Extensional:
    agreement index, 66–67
    attitude, 66
    meaning, 65
Extremity effect, 62

Feedback:
    delay of, 9
    as knowledge of results, 8
    proprioceptive, 37, 44
Festinger, L., 102–104, 114
Fivel, H. W., 48, 116
Fixation and problem solving, 96–100, 104

Fixation (continued)
drive level, 97–98, 100, 104
past experience, 98–99
Fleming, W. H., 103, 113
Flesch, R., 70, 114
Forgetting:
and disuse, 19–20, 33
and organization, 21–22, 33
Franklin, M., 33, 115
Freud, S., 30–31

General semantics, 65–67, 78
Generalization, 3
and cognition, 40–41
stimulus, 35–39
response, 39–40, 110
Gestalt, 26, 81
Glanzer, M., 23–24, 114
Gleason, T. G., 62, 116
Glucksberg, S., 97–98, 114
Goldstein, L. S., 14, 114
Goodnow, J. J., 54, 113
Gormezano, I., 50, 114
Goranson, R. E., 76, 113
Gotkin, L. G., 14, 114
Grant, D. A., 50, 114
Greenspoon, J., 11–12, 114
Guthrie, E. R., 39, 114

Habit-family hierarchy:
in learning, 5, 15
in problem solving, 96, 97
Harlow, H. F., 83–85, 103, 114
Harvey, O. J., 72, 114
Heise, G. A., 68, 116
Highes, R. H., 39, 117
Hilgard, E. R., 108, 114
Hoffman, L. R., 110, 114
Hogan, H. P., 25, 113
Horton, H. P., 39, 114
Hovland, C. I., 72, 114
Howe, E. S., 63, 115
Hull, C. L., 46, 115
Hunter, W. S., 92–93, 115
Hypothesis and evidence, 2

Implicit (or subvocal) speech, 85–86
Insight, 80–85, 103–104
Intensional agreement, 67
Interpreting persuasive messages, 71–76, 79
Intraverbal behavior, 59
Introspection, 1
Involvement, 76–77

Jacobovits, L. A., 64, 115
Jenkins, J. G., 27–28, 115
Johnson, W., 66, 115
Judson, A. I., 101, 115

Kalish, H. I., 56, 113
Katona, G., 41, 115
Kendler, H. H., 28, 52, 115
Kendler, T. S., 52, 115
Knowledge of results, 8–10, 16 (see also Feedback)

Köhler, W., 81–82, 103, 115
Korzybski, A., 65, 115

Lambert, W. E., 64, 115
Language, 56–79
productive character, 67–68
Lantz, D., 89, 115
Law of effect, 10, 16 (see also Reinforcement)
Law of least effort, 70–71, 87
Lawless, R. H., 26, 114
Learning, 4–17
definition, 4
ease of and forgetting, 2
incidental, 10–11
latent, 7–8
to learn, 84
and meaning, 59–60
and performance, 8, 16
programmed, 12–15
set, 83–85
and thinking, 81
Lehman, H. C., 107–108, 115
Lenneberg, E. H., 88–89, 113
Lewis, H. B., 33, 115
Lichter, W., 68, 116
Luchins, A. S., 99–100, 115
Luchins, E. S., 99, 115

Maier, N. R. F., 83, 101, 110, 114–115, 116
Maltzman, I., 110, 116
Mand, 58
Manis, M., 62, 72, 75, 116
Marshall, R. W., 26, 114
Max, L. W., 85–86
Meaning, 59, 78
connotative, 60–62, 78
denotative, 60–61
extensional, 65, 78
intensional, 65, 79
lexical, 67
linguistic, 67
structural, 67
Meaning response (r_m), 37 (see also Mediation)
Mediating response, 60, 65
Mediation:
and concept formation, 44
and generalization, 36–37
Mednick, S. A., 111–112, 116
Memory, 18–34
and codability, 88–89
and motivation, 30
and organization, 21–25
trace, 26
Method of savings, 18–19
Miller, G. A., 21–22, 67, 68, 70, 116
Miller, N. E., 94–95, 114
Mills, J., 102, 116
Mischel, W., 93, 116
Motivation:
and cognitive dissonance, 102–103
and delayed feedback, 10
and memory, 30
and problem solving, 97–98, 100

Mowrer, C. H., 63, 64

Nonsense syllable, 18–19

Organization:
 and memory, 21, 30
 and memory distortion, 24–26
Originality:
 and creativity, 105
 stimulation of, 110–111
Osborn, A. F., 109, 116
Osgood, C. E., 59–65, 116
Osler, S. F., 48, 116

Perspective effect, 77
Postman, L., 10, 116
Pressey, S. L., 12
Proactive inhibition, 29–30, 34
Problem solving, 80–102
 and diversity of group members, 110
Proprioceptive feedback, 37, 44, 59, 60
 (see also Mediation)
Proprioceptor, 37
Psychotherapy and semantic differential, 63
Punishment, 6
 and memory, 19–20

Readability, 69–70
Reading, 6
 as textual behavior, 59
Redundancy, 68–69
Reinforcement, 5–8, 15
 and language, 56
 mechanistic versus cognitive effects, 10–12, 16
Relevant and irrelevant cues, 46
Remote associates test (RAT) 111–112
Representation:
 in animals, 92–93
 of future, 93–94
 and thought, 91–96
Repression, 30–32, 34
Response, 5
 generalization, 35, 39–40, 43
  acquired, 39
  and originality, 110
  primary, 39
 light-weight, 59
 observable, 85
 specific versus response clusters, 39–40
 as symbolic process, 91
Response-produced stimulus (s_m), 37
 (see also Mediation and Proprioceptive feedback)
Restructuring problems:
 and hints, 101
 and rewording, 100
 through varied sequence, 101
Retention, 19–20
Retroactive inhibition, 27, 34
Rosenzweig, S., 33, 117

Sapir, E., 71, 117

Self (or ego) orientation, 33
Selfridge, J. A., 21, 116
Semantic differential, 60–65
Semantic satiation, 64
Semantics, 59, 67, 79
Sherif, M., 72, 114
Sign learning, 59
Silverman, R. E., 14, 114
Skinner, B. F., 12, 14, 17, 56–59, 78, 117
Socratic method, 14
Sorting tests, 42
Spielberger, C. D., 57, 117
Stagner, R., 117
Stefflre, V., 89, 115
Stimulus, 5, 35
 generalization, 35–40, 43
  mediated, 36–39
  primary, 35
 observable, 85
 similarity and retroactive inhibition, 27–29
 as symbolic process, 91
Subvocal speech, 85–86, 104
Successive approximations, 14, 17
Suci, G., 61, 116
Syntactics, 67–70, 79

Tact, 58
Task orientation, 33
Tannenbaum, P., 61, 116
Taylor, W. L., 69, 117
Textual behavior, 59
Theories, 4
Thinking:
 central neural mechanisms, 86
 and insight, 81–85
 and language, 85–91
 learning and, 81
 and peripheral motor activity, 86
 productive, 80–81
 reproductive, 80
Thistlethwaite, D., 102, 117
Thorndike, E. L., 8, 10, 16, 81, 82, 117
Thought:
 and language, 85–95, 104
 and motivation, 102–103
 and representation, 91
Thruston, J. R., 56, 113
Trabasso, T., 49, 113
Trautman, G. E., 48, 116

Underwood, B. J., 30, 39, 117

Verbal behavior, 56–57
Vocabulary, 87–91
Vocal behavior, 57

Walker, E. L., 26, 117
Walter, A. A., 25, 113
Ward, C. D., 76, 117
Watson, J. B., 85, 104
Whorf, B. L., 86–91, 104
Whorfian hypothesis, 86–91

Woodworth, R. S., 20
Word:
  familiarity, 69
  frequency, 70, 79
  length, 70, 79
  order, 67–70, 79

Wundt, W., 6

Zeigarnik, B., 32, 117
Zeigarnik effect, 32–34
Zeller, A. F., 31, 117
Zipf, G. K., 70, 79, 87–88, 117

DATE DUE